Quick
Scripture
Reference
for
Counseling
Women

Quick Scripture Reference for Counseling Women

PATRICIA MILLER

Baker Books

A Division of Baker Book House Co
Grand Rapids, Michigan 49516

© 2002 by Patricia Miller

Published by Baker Books
a division of Baker Publishing Group
P.O. Box 6287, Grand Rapids, MI 49516-6287
www.bakerbooks.com

Seventh printing, June 2008

Printed in the United States of America

ISBN 978-0-8010-9138-4

Subject Guide

Introduction

Purpose of This Book

While all Scripture is profitable to both men and women, there are special needs and concerns that women face. As a result, counselors, pastors, and those who guide women need to be prepared to use Scripture that can encourage and comfort those individuals who struggle with life's complexities.

> All Scripture is God-breathed and is useful for teaching, rebuking, correcting and training in righteousness, so that the man of God may be thoroughly equipped for every good work.
>
> 2 Timothy 3:16–17

Though this book covers needs specific to women, it also covers many general areas with which both men and women can identify. However, even in those general areas, verses were chosen as to touch a woman's heart and were particularly studied from a woman's point of view. The desire is that this book will be a tool and at least a beginning point of further study of Scripture that can be used for each area of need.

Counseling is a work of the heart. The biblical principles of God's Word affect both the heart of the counselor and the heart of the one counseled. The goal is to guide troubled individuals, whatever their problem, into confidence in God and his Word. Herein lies the true value and success of biblical counseling, and discipling. While the world offers theories, programs, and steps to follow, they again belong to the world. We cannot be totally confident that they are right or even helpful to follow. Everything must pass through the lens of Scripture and only then can it be used. Never has there been such confidence, excitement, and freedom as when the Word of God is used. One does not have to wonder, "Will this work?" God's Word in a teachable heart can go far beyond any counselor's words. Scripture is always sufficient for any area of life. Every problem, every need, every hurt or desire can be met by Scripture. While Scripture might not specifically address a particular issue, the principles are valid to help an individual in every situation.

Isaiah 61:1–3 summarizes the goal for counseling in a beautiful way. Although given to the prophet toward Israel, the principle is relevant for today.

The Spirit of the Sovereign LORD is on me, because the LORD has anointed me to preach good news to the poor. He has sent me to bind up the brokenhearted, to proclaim freedom for the captives and release from darkness for the prisoners, to proclaim the year of the LORD's favor and the day of vengeance of our God, to comfort all who mourn, and provide for those who grieve in Zion—to bestow on them a crown of beauty instead of ashes, the oil of gladness instead of mourning, and a garment of praise instead of a spirit of despair. They will be called oaks of righteousness, a planting of the LORD for the display of his splendor.

How to Use This Book

There are seventy-five different topics listed in alphabetical order that are addressed in this book. The first topic is a guide for the Plan of Salvation with supporting Scripture. It is vital that a biblical counselor be prepared to lead individuals to a personal relationship with Jesus Christ as Savior and on to a deeper relationship as Lord of their lives. It is so vital that before any counseling problems are addressed this issue should first be evaluated; therefore the significance of this first topic.

As a counseling session is planned and topics are identified, the counselor can prepare a list of pages and also numbered points from those pages of significant Scriptures that are appropriate. Topics are also cross-referenced to each other. For example, someone looking up Mothering would also see under that heading a suggestion to look up the topics Disciplining Children and Training Children.

Homework is another way to assist counselees. Give them Scripture for study and interaction throughout the week. (What spoke to them? What applies? What do they want to ignore? What verses could they add? What did God say? What should they do?)

My desire is that this book of Scripture, organized by topic, will influence both your life and mine, and that as God brings those in need into our lives we will be able to better show them the Savior and strengthen their walk with their Lord.

My prayer is that the reality of Deuteronomy 32:4 will be true in our lives: *They* (God's Words) *are not just idle words for you—they are your life.* May it ever be so!

Plan of Salvation

Always crucial to any counseling is the need to ascertain if the individual has a personal relationship with Jesus Christ. If not, the counselor's first task is to guide the counselee to such a relationship. Only then will the Scripture, with the power of the Holy Spirit, be able to truly do its work.

Steps in guiding an individual to Christ (If possible, have counselees read the passages themselves from a Bible.)

1. **Each person is separated from God because of sin and sinful behavior.**

    Romans 3:23 For all have sinned and fall short of the glory of God.

    Isaiah 53:6 We all, like sheep, have gone astray, each of us has turned to his own way; and the LORD has laid on him the iniquity of us all.

2. **Sin must be punished—separation from God, hell.**

    Romans 6:23 For the wages of sin is death, but the gift of God is eternal life in Christ Jesus our Lord.

3. **There is nothing a person can do to gain status with God or to earn merit toward salvation.**

    Ephesians 2:8–9 For it is by grace you have been saved, through faith—and this not from yourselves, it is the gift of God—not by works, so that no one can boast.

    Titus 3:5 He saved us, not because of righteous things we had done, but because of his mercy. He saved us through the washing of rebirth and renewal by the Holy Spirit.

> **Isaiah 64:6** All of us have become like one who is unclean, and all our righteous acts are like filthy rags; we all shrivel up like a leaf, and like the wind our sins sweep us away.

4. Recognizing this dilemma, God had in place from creation a way for an individual to have a personal relationship with himself. The way was through the death of his son, Jesus Christ.

> **Romans 5:8** But God demonstrates his own love for us in this: While we were still sinners, Christ died for us.

> **John 3:16** For God so loved the world that he gave his one and only Son, that whoever believes in him shall not perish but have eternal life.

> **Romans 10:9** That if you confess with your mouth, "Jesus is Lord," and believe in your heart that God raised him from the dead, you will be saved.

5. Each person must repent of their sin and personally believe (i.e. trust) in Jesus Christ as the only way to receive God's forgiveness to gain entrance into heaven.

> **John 1:12** Yet to all who received him, to those who believed in his name, he gave the right to become children of God.

> **John 3:36** Whoever believes in the Son has eternal life, but whoever rejects the Son will not see life, for God's wrath remains on him.

> **Luke 15:7, 10** I tell you that in the same way there will be more rejoicing in heaven over one sinner who repents than over ninety-nine righteous persons who do not need to repent. . . . In the same way, I tell you, there is rejoicing in the presence of the angels of God over one sinner who repents.

6. Salvation is assured.

> **1 John 5:13** I write these things to you who believe in the name of the Son of God so that you may know that you have eternal life.

> **John 5:24** I tell you the truth, whoever hears my word and believes him who sent me has eternal life and will not be condemned; he has crossed over from death to life.

Abortion

Preventing an Abortion

1. God is actively and personally involved in the unborn's life, down to planning each day of his/her life.

   Psalm 139:13–16 For you created my inmost being; you knit me together in my mother's womb. I praise you because I am fearfully and wonderfully made; your works are wonderful, I know that full well. My frame was not hidden from you when I was made in the secret place. When I was woven together in the depths of the earth, your eyes saw my unformed body. All the days ordained for me were written in your book before one of them came to be.

2. Birth is not the origin of life; it is the arrival.

   Psalm 139:16 Your eyes saw my unformed body. All the days ordained for me were written in your book before one of them came to be.

3. Following what self wants, rather than what God wants, leads to future problems.

   Proverbs 14:12 There is a way that seems right to a man, but in the end it leads to death.

   Proverbs 12:15 The way of a fool seems right to him, but a wise man listens to advice.

   Proverbs 16:2 All a man's ways seem innocent to him, but motives are weighed by the LORD.

Colossians 1:9–10 For this reason, since the day we heard about you, we have not stopped praying for you and asking God to fill you with the knowledge of his will through all spiritual wisdom and understanding. And we pray this in order that you may live a life worthy of the Lord and may please him in every way: bearing fruit in every good work, growing in the knowledge of God.

Philippians 1:9–10 And this is my prayer: that your love may abound more and more in knowledge and depth of insight, so that you may be able to discern what is best and may be pure and blameless until the day of Christ.

4. Elizabeth's unborn baby was aware of the unborn child Mary carried. Though a unique situation (God/man in the womb) it gives evidence of personhood in the womb.

Luke 1:44 As soon as the sound of your greeting reached my ears, the baby in my womb leaped for joy.

5. Our actions are not hidden from God.

Hebrews 4:13 Nothing in all creation is hidden from God's sight. Everything is uncovered and laid bare before the eyes of him to whom we must give account.

6. Self may desire to get out of a pregnancy, but that is not what God desires. Choosing God's way, no matter how difficult, leads to life and peace.

Romans 8:5–6 Those who live according to the sinful nature have their minds set on what that nature desires; but those who live in accordance with the Spirit have their minds set on what the Spirit desires. The mind of sinful man is death, but the mind controlled by the Spirit is life and peace.

7. The prophets recognized that God knew them as unborn.

Jeremiah 1:5 Before I formed you in the womb I knew you, before you were born I set you apart; I appointed you as a prophet to the nations.

Isaiah 49:1 Listen to me, you islands; hear this, you distant nations: Before I was born the LORD called me; from my birth he has made mention of my name.

8. **Children are a reward—a gift from God—no matter how their conception began.**

    Psalm 127:3–4 Sons are a heritage from the LORD, children a reward from him. Like arrows in the hands of a warrior are sons born in one's youth.

9. **Our bodies are not ours—they belong to God.**

    2 Corinthians 6:16 What agreement is there between the temple of God and idols? For we are the temple of the living God. As God has said: "I will live with them and walk among them, and I will be their God, and they will be my people."

    1 Corinthians 6:19 Do you not know that your body is a temple of the Holy Spirit, who is in you, whom you have received from God? You are not your own.

    1 Corinthians 3:16 Don't you know that you yourselves are God's temple and that God's Spirit lives in you?

    Romans 12:1–2 Therefore, I urge you, brothers, in view of God's mercy, to offer your bodies as living sacrifices, holy and pleasing to God—this is your spiritual act of worship. Do not conform any longer to the pattern of this world, but be transformed by the renewing of your mind. Then you will be able to test and approve what God's will is—his good, pleasing and perfect will.

After an Abortion (See also Forgiveness)

1. **When forgiveness is requested, it is granted without reservation.**

    Psalm 32:3–5 When I kept silent, my bones wasted away through my groaning all day long. For day and night your hand was heavy upon me; my strength was sapped as in the heat of summer. Then I acknowledged my sin to you and did not cover up my iniquity. I said,

"I will confess my transgressions to the LORD"—and you forgave the guilt of my sin.

2. **God can take our broken spirit and produce joy.**

   Psalm 51:10–17 Create in me a pure heart, O God, and renew a steadfast spirit within me. Do not cast me from your presence or take your Holy Spirit from me. Restore to me the joy of your salvation and grant me a willing spirit, to sustain me. Then I will teach transgressors your ways, and sinners will turn back to you. Save me from bloodguilt, O God, the God who saves me, and my tongue will sing of your righteousness. O Lord, open my lips, and my mouth will declare your praise. You do not delight in sacrifice, or I would bring it; you do not take pleasure in burnt offerings. The sacrifices of God are a broken spirit; a broken and contrite heart, O God, you will not despise.

3. **God offers restoration.**

   Psalm 40:1–3 I waited patiently for the LORD; he turned to me and heard my cry. He lifted me out of the slimy pit, out of the mud and mire; he set my feet on a rock and gave me a firm place to stand. He put a new song in my mouth, a hymn of praise to our God. Many will see and fear and put their trust in the LORD.

4. **God understands the women of Israel weeping for children they would never see again—He understands sorrow for loss of children.**

   Jeremiah 31:15 This is what the LORD says: "A voice is heard in Ramah, mourning and great weeping, Rachel weeping for her children and refusing to be comforted, because her children are no more."

   Matthew 2:17–18 Then what was said through the prophet Jeremiah was fulfilled: "A voice is heard in Ramah, weeping and great mourning, Rachel weeping for her children and refusing to be comforted, because they are no more."

5. **As those in Israel's captivity were not to dwell on the awfulness of the captivity, so we are also not to dwell on the past once it is forgiven.**

   Isaiah 43:18–19 Forget the former things; do not dwell on the past. See, I am doing a new thing! Now it springs up; do you not perceive it? I am making a way in the desert and streams in the wasteland.

6. **God is the only one who can save us from our sorrow.**

Psalm 18:1–6 I love you, O LORD, my strength. The LORD is my rock, my fortress and my deliverer; my God is my rock, in whom I take refuge. He is my shield and the horn of my salvation, my stronghold. I call to the LORD, who is worthy of praise, and I am saved from my enemies. The cords of death entangled me; the torrents of destruction overwhelmed me. The cords of the grave coiled around me; the snares of death confronted me. In my distress I called to the LORD; I cried to my God for help. From his temple he heard my voice; my cry came before him, into his ears.

Isaiah 25:8 The Sovereign LORD will wipe away the tears from all faces; he will remove the disgrace of his people from all the earth. The LORD has spoken.

Abuse

See also Trials, Past Memories

Help for the Abused

1. God is our refuge.

Psalm 17:8–9 Keep me as the apple of your eye; hide me in the shadow of your wings from the wicked who assail me, from my mortal enemies who surround me.

Isaiah 25:4 You have been a refuge for the poor, a refuge for the needy in his distress, a shelter from the storm and a shade from the heat. For the breath of the ruthless is like a storm driving against a wall.

Jeremiah 17:17 Do not be a terror to me; you are my refuge in the day of disaster.

2. The Lord Jesus, himself, was to experience great abuse.

Isaiah 53:5–6 But he was pierced for our transgressions, he was crushed for our iniquities; the punishment that brought us peace was upon him, and by his wounds we are healed. We all, like sheep, have gone astray, each of us has turned to his own way; and the LORD has laid on him the iniquity of us all.

3. **When we feel alone, God is there, and we can call on him.**

   Psalm 142:1–7 I cry aloud to the LORD; I lift up my voice to the LORD for mercy. I pour out my complaint before him; before him I tell my trouble. When my spirit grows faint within me, it is you who know my way. In the path where I walk men have hidden a snare for me. Look to my right and see; no one is concerned for me. I have no refuge; no one cares for my life. I cry to you, O LORD; I say, "You are my refuge, my portion in the land of the living." Listen to my cry, for I am in desperate need; rescue me from those who pursue me, for they are too strong for me. Set me free from my prison, that I may praise your name. Then the righteous will gather about me because of your goodness to me.

4. **Although we do not know when or how God will rescue, in some way he will provide the strength.**

   Psalm 72:12 For he will deliver the needy who cry out, the afflicted who have no one to help.

   Psalm 107:19–20 Then they cried to the LORD in their trouble, and he saved them from their distress. He sent forth his word and healed them; he rescued them from the grave.

   Psalm 144:7 Reach down your hand from on high; deliver me and rescue me from the mighty waters, from the hands of foreigners.

5. **David prayed for safety from evil men—we can do the same.**

   Psalm 140:1–13 Rescue me, O LORD, from evil men; protect me from men of violence, who devise evil plans in their hearts and stir up war every day. They make their tongues as sharp as a serpent's; the poison of vipers is on their lips. Keep me, O LORD, from the hands of the wicked; protect me from men of violence who plan to trip my feet. Proud men have hidden a snare for me; they have spread out the cords of their net and have set traps for me along my path. O LORD, I say to you, "You are my God." Hear, O LORD, my cry for mercy. O Sovereign LORD, my strong deliverer, who shields my head in the day of battle—do not grant the wicked their desires, O LORD; do not let their plans succeed, or they will become proud. Let the heads of those who surround me be covered with the trouble their lips have caused. Let burning coals fall upon them; may they be thrown into the fire, into miry pits, never to rise. Let slanderers not be established in the land; may disaster hunt down men of violence. I know that the LORD secures justice for the poor and upholds the cause of the needy. Surely the righteous will praise your name and the upright will live before you.

6. Do not allow past fears to control present life—when there is nothing we can do to correct the past we must trust it to God's future care.

   Isaiah 43:18–19 Forget the former things; do not dwell on the past. See, I am doing a new thing! Now it springs up; do you not perceive it? I am making a way in the desert and streams in the wasteland.

   Philippians 3:13 Brothers, I do not consider myself yet to have taken hold of it. But one thing I do: Forgetting what is behind and straining toward what is ahead . . .

   Matthew 10:26 So do not be afraid of them. There is nothing concealed that will not be disclosed, or hidden that will not be made known.

Comfort for the Abused

1. Our God who is sovereign over our past can help us today.

   Psalm 103:3–11 Who forgives all your sins and heals all your diseases, who redeems your life from the pit and crowns you with love and compassion, who satisfies your desires with good things so that your youth is renewed like the eagle's. The LORD works righteousness and justice for all the oppressed. He made known his ways to Moses, his deeds to the people of Israel: The LORD is compassionate and gracious, slow to anger, abounding in love. He will not always accuse, nor will he harbor his anger forever; he does not treat us as our sins deserve or repay us according to our iniquities. For as high as the heavens are above the earth, so great is his love for those who fear him.

2. **Although the Thessalonian Christians were suffering, they had joy in spite of suffering and were examples as believers.**

   1 Thessalonians 1:6–7 You became imitators of us and of the Lord; in spite of severe suffering, you welcomed the message with the joy given by the Holy Spirit. And so you became a model to all the believers in Macedonia and Achaia.

3. **We can always talk to God about the problem.**

   Hebrews 4:16 Let us then approach the throne of grace with confidence, so that we may receive mercy and find grace to help us in our time of need.

4. **God is sufficient to give us strength through trials.**

   2 Corinthians 12:9–10 But he said to me, "My grace is sufficient for you, for my power is made perfect in weakness." Therefore I will boast all the more gladly about my weaknesses, so that Christ's power may rest on me. That is why, for Christ's sake, I delight in weaknesses, in insults, in hardships, in persecutions, in difficulties. For when I am weak, then I am strong.

NOTE: It would be beneficial to have the counselee see a physician.

Adoption

See also Orphan

1. **Esther, raised by her cousin, was instrumental in saving the Jewish nation.**

   Esther 2:15 When the turn came for Esther (the girl Mordecai had adopted, the daughter of his uncle Abihail) to go to the king, she asked for nothing other than what Hegai, the king's eunuch who was in charge of the harem, suggested. And Esther won the favor of everyone who saw her.

   Esther 4:14 For if you remain silent at this time, relief and deliverance for the Jews will arise from another place, but you and your father's family will perish. And who knows but that you have come to royal position for such a time as this?

2. **God looks favorably on those who care for orphans.**

   James 1:27 Religion that God our Father accepts as pure and faultless is this: to look after orphans and widows in their distress and to keep oneself from being polluted by the world.

3. **God adopts us into his family at salvation.**

   Galatians 4:7 So you are no longer a slave, but a son; and since you are a son, God has made you also an heir.

Romans 8:23 Not only so, but we ourselves, who have the firstfruits of the Spirit, groan inwardly as we wait eagerly for our adoption as sons, the redemption of our bodies.

Ephesians 1:5 He predestined us to be adopted as his sons through Jesus Christ, in accordance with his pleasure and will.

4. **Whether with a biological family or adopted family, God is intimately involved in that life.**

Jeremiah 29:11 "For I know the plans I have for you," declares the LORD, "plans to prosper you and not to harm you, plans to give you hope and a future."

Psalm 139:16 Your eyes saw my unformed body. All the days ordained for me were written in your book before one of them came to be.

Adultery

See also Sexual Purity, Temptation

1. **Adultery is being sexually involved with someone outside the bonds of marriage.**

   Proverbs 5:20 Why be captivated, my son, by an adulteress? Why embrace the bosom of another man's wife?

2. **Lustful thinking—imagining what it would be like—is mental and emotional adultery—***sin.*

   Matthew 5:28 But I tell you that anyone who looks at a woman lustfully has already committed adultery with her in his heart.

3. **You must not take what belongs to another—another's mate.**

   Exodus 20:15 You shall not steal.

   Exodus 20:17 You shall not covet your neighbor's house. You shall not covet your neighbor's wife, or his manservant or maidservant, his ox or donkey, or anything that belongs to your neighbor.

   1 Thessalonians 4:6 And that in this matter no one should wrong his brother or take advantage of him. The Lord will punish men for all such sins, as we have already told you and warned you.

4. **God commands: No adultery—it is his law.**

   Exodus 20:14 You shall not commit adultery.

5. **Adultery, like all sin, separates us from God. Only Jesus Christ offers us release.**

   1 Corinthians 6:9–11 Do you not know that the wicked will not inherit the kingdom of God? Do not be deceived: Neither the sexually immoral nor idolaters nor adulterers nor male prostitutes nor homosexual offenders nor thieves nor the greedy nor drunkards nor slanderers nor swindlers will inherit the kingdom of God. And that is what some of you were. But you were washed, you were sanctified, you were justified in the name of the Lord Jesus Christ and by the Spirit of our God.

6. **Adultery is caused when a person's inner compass is not focused on God.**

   Matthew 15:19 For out of the heart come evil thoughts, murder, adultery, sexual immorality, theft, false testimony, slander.

7. **Adultery is stopped by changing our mental view and seeing it from God's view.**

   Romans 8:5–6 Those who live according to the sinful nature have their minds set on what that nature desires; but those who live in accordance with the Spirit have their minds set on what the Spirit desires. The mind of sinful man is death, but the mind controlled by the Spirit is life and peace.

   Romans 12:1–2 Therefore, I urge you, brothers, in view of God's mercy, to offer your bodies as living sacrifices, holy and pleasing to God—this is your spiritual act of worship. Do not conform any longer to the pattern of this world, but be transformed by the renewing of your mind. Then you will be able to test and approve what God's will is—his good, pleasing and perfect will.

8. **God's wisdom—his Word—can save from adultery.**

   Proverbs 2:16–18 It will save you also from the adulteress, from the wayward wife with her seductive words, who has left the partner of her youth and ignored the covenant she made before God. For her house leads down to death and her paths to the spirits of the dead.

9. **Adultery always has great consequences leading to destruction.**

   Proverbs 6:27–29, 32 Can a man scoop fire into his lap without his clothes being burned? Can a man walk on hot coals without his feet being scorched? So is he who sleeps with another man's wife; no one who touches her will go unpunished. . . . But a man who commits adultery lacks judgment; whoever does so destroys himself.

   Proverbs 5:20–23 Why be captivated, my son, by an adulteress? Why embrace the bosom of another man's wife? For a man's ways are in full view of the LORD, and he examines all his paths. The evil deeds of a wicked man ensnare him; the cords of his sin hold him fast. He will die for lack of discipline, led astray by his own great folly.

10. **An individual has no right to separate what God has placed together.**

    Mark 10:8–9 And the two will become one flesh. So they are no longer two, but one. Therefore what God has joined together, let man not separate.

11. **Steps for preventing adultery.**

    1 Corinthians 7:3–5 The husband should fulfill his marital duty to his wife, and likewise the wife to her husband. The wife's body does not belong to her alone but also to her husband. In the same way, the husband's body does not belong to him alone but also to his wife. Do not deprive each other except by mutual consent and for a time, so that you may devote yourselves to prayer. Then come together again so that Satan will not tempt you because of your lack of self-control.

    1 Thessalonians 4:3–5 It is God's will that you should be sanctified: that you should avoid sexual immorality; that each of you should learn to control his own body in a way that is holy and honorable, not in passionate lust like the heathen, who do not know God.

12. **Sex with your own spouse is to be desired and enjoyed; it is recreational.**

    Proverbs 5:15–19 Drink water from your own cistern, running water from your own well. Should your springs overflow in the streets, your streams of water in the public squares? Let them be yours alone, never to be shared with strangers. May your fountain be blessed, and may you rejoice in the wife of your youth. A loving doe, a graceful deer—may her breasts satisfy you always, may you ever be captivated by her love.

Book of Song of Solomon

Alcohol/Drug Abuse

See also Temptation

1. **Alcohol and drugs are harmful to the body God created.**

   1 Corinthians 6:19 Do you not know that your body is a temple of the Holy Spirit, who is in you, whom you have received from God? You are not your own.

2. **We are commanded to be controlled by the Spirit, not human substitutes.**

   Ephesians 5:18 Do not get drunk on wine, which leads to debauchery. Instead, be filled with the Spirit.

3. **Drunken behavior is sinful and separates us from God.**

   Galatians 5:19–21 The acts of the sinful nature are obvious: sexual immorality, impurity and debauchery; idolatry and witchcraft; hatred, discord, jealousy, fits of rage, selfish ambition, dissensions, factions and envy; drunkenness, orgies, and the like. I warn you, as I did before, that those who live like this will not inherit the kingdom of God.

   1 Corinthians 6:9–11 Do not be deceived: Neither the sexually immoral nor idolaters nor adulterers nor male prostitutes nor homosexual offenders nor thieves nor the greedy nor drunkards nor slanderers nor swindlers will inherit the kingdom of God. And that is what some of you were. But you were washed, you were sanctified, you were justified in the name of the Lord Jesus Christ and by the Spirit of our God.

4. **Drunken behavior is not an option for the child of God.**

Romans 13:13–14 Let us behave decently, as in the daytime, not in orgies and drunkenness, not in sexual immorality and debauchery, not in dissension and jealousy. Rather, clothe yourselves with the Lord Jesus Christ, and do not think about how to gratify the desires of the sinful nature.

1 Peter 4:1–3 Therefore, since Christ suffered in his body, arm yourselves also with the same attitude, because he who has suffered in his body is done with sin. As a result, he does not live the rest of his earthly life for evil human desires, but rather for the will of God. For you have spent enough time in the past doing what pagans choose to do—living in debauchery, lust, drunkenness, orgies, carousing and detestable idolatry.

Isaiah 5:11–12, 22 Woe to those who rise early in the morning to run after their drinks, who stay up late at night till they are inflamed with wine. They have harps and lyres at their banquets, tambourines and flutes and wine, but they have no regard for the deeds of the LORD, no respect for the work of his hands. . . . Woe to those who are heroes at drinking wine and champions at mixing drinks.

Habakkuk 2:15–16 Woe to him who gives drink to his neighbors, pouring it from the wineskin till they are drunk, so that he can gaze on their naked bodies. You will be filled with shame instead of glory. Now it is your turn! Drink and be exposed! The cup from the LORD's right hand is coming around to you, and disgrace will cover your glory.

5. **There is hope for change from this habit.**

1 Corinthians 6:9–11 Do you not know that the wicked will not inherit the kingdom of God? Do not be deceived: Neither the sexually immoral nor idolaters nor adulterers nor male prostitutes nor homosexual offenders nor thieves nor the greedy nor drunkards nor slanderers nor swindlers will inherit the kingdom of God. And that is what some of you were. But you were washed, you were sanctified, you were justified in the name of the Lord Jesus Christ and by the Spirit of our God.

6. **Leaders in ministry cannot be given to drunkenness.**

   1 Timothy 3:2–3 Now the overseer must be above reproach, the husband of but one wife, temperate, self-controlled, respectable, hospitable, able to teach, not given to drunkenness, not violent but gentle, not quarrelsome, not a lover of money.

   Titus 1:7 Since an overseer is entrusted with God's work, he must be blameless—not overbearing, not quick-tempered, not given to drunkenness, not violent, not pursuing dishonest gain.

7. **Associations with drunkenness that are not attractive.**
   Genesis 9:21—exposure, nakedness
   Job 12:25—staggering
   Psalm 107:27—reeling, staggering, at wits' end
   Proverbs 23:21—poverty, drowsiness
   Isaiah 19:14—staggering in vomit
   Isaiah 24:20—reeling, swaying, and falling
   Jeremiah 25:27—vomiting
   Lamentations 4:21—stripped naked
   Ezekiel 23:33—ruin, desolation
   Romans 13:13—indecent behavior
   Ephesians 5:18—debauchery

NOTE: It may be beneficial to have the counselee see a physician.

Anger

Becoming Angry

Righteous Anger/Indignation

1. **God himself expresses righteous anger against sin.**

   Exodus 32:10

   Ezekiel 23:25

   Jeremiah 6:11

2. **Jesus expressed righteous anger.**

   Mark 11:15 (In the temple)

   Matthew 21:12–13 (In the temple)

   Mark 3:5 He looked around at them in anger and, deeply distressed at their stubborn hearts . . .

3. **The believer can also express righteous anger.**

   Ephesians 4:26 "In your anger do not sin": Do not let the sun go down while you are still angry.

Unrighteous Anger

1. **Anger is included in a list of disgusting sins.**

   Galatians 5:19–21 The acts of the sinful nature are obvious: sexual immorality, impurity and debauchery; idolatry and witchcraft; hatred, discord, jealousy, fits of rage, selfish ambition, dissensions, factions and envy; drunkenness, orgies, and the like. I warn you, as I did before, that those who live like this will not inherit the kingdom of God.

Proverbs 29:22 An angry man stirs up dissension, and a hot-tempered one commits many sins.

2. **No option—anger has to be removed.**

Colossians 3:8 But now you must rid yourselves of all such things as these: anger, rage, malice, slander, and filthy language from your lips.

Ephesians 4:31–32 Get rid of all bitterness, rage and anger, brawling and slander, along with every form of malice. Be kind and compassionate to one another, forgiving each other, just as in Christ God forgave you.

3. **Anger is loss of control.**

Proverbs 29:11 A fool gives full vent to his anger, but a wise man keeps himself under control.

Jonah 4:4, 9 But the LORD replied, "Have you any right to be angry?". . . But God said to Jonah, "Do you have a right to be angry about the vine?" "I do," he said. "I am angry enough to die."

4. **Avoiding anger requires proceeding slowly, not reacting.**

Proverbs 14:17 A quick-tempered man does foolish things, and a crafty man is hated.

Proverbs 20:3 It is to a man's honor to avoid strife, but every fool is quick to quarrel.

5. **Listen more, talk less, slow down anger.**

James 1:19–20 My dear brothers, take note of this: Everyone should be quick to listen, slow to speak and slow to become angry, for man's anger does not bring about the righteous life that God desires.

Responding to anger

1. **The practice of answering gently will for the most part reduce the chance of anger.**

   Proverbs 15:1 A gentle answer turns away wrath, but a harsh word stirs up anger.

2. **Do not respond to anger with anger.**

   Romans 12:19 Do not take revenge, my friends, but leave room for God's wrath, for it is written: "It is mine to avenge; I will repay," says the Lord.

   Proverbs 20:22 Do not say, "I'll pay you back for this wrong!" Wait for the LORD, and he will deliver you.

3. **If anger is expressed it must be taken care of that day between individuals and God, or at the very least a conscious plan must be made that day for resolution.**

   Ephesians 4:26 "In your anger do not sin": Do not let the sun go down while you are still angry.

   Psalm 4:4 In your anger do not sin; when you are on your beds, search your hearts and be silent.

4. **Patience—the contrast to anger.**

   Proverbs 14:29 A patient man has great understanding, but a quick-tempered man displays folly.

   Proverbs 15:18 A hot-tempered man stirs up dissension, but a patient man calms a quarrel.

   Proverbs 16:32 Better a patient man than a warrior, a man who controls his temper than one who takes a city.

5. **Look out for anger in choosing friends or a mate.**

   Proverbs 19:19 A hot-tempered man must pay the penalty; if you rescue him, you will have to do it again.

   Proverbs 22:24 Do not make friends with a hot-tempered man, do not associate with one easily angered.

Anxiety/Worry

1. **The result of anxiety.**

   Proverbs 12:25 An anxious heart weighs a man down, but a kind word cheers him up.

2. **Proper response to anxiety.**

   1 Peter 5:7 Cast all your anxiety on him because he cares for you.

   Philippians 4:6–7 Do not be anxious about anything, but in everything, by prayer and petition, with thanksgiving, present your requests to God. And the peace of God, which transcends all understanding, will guard your hearts and your minds in Christ Jesus.

   Isaiah 41:10, 13 So do not fear, for I am with you; do not be dismayed, for I am your God. I will strengthen you and help you; I will uphold you with my righteous right hand. . . . For I am the LORD, your God, who takes hold of your right hand and says to you, Do not fear; I will help you.

3. **Anxiety is often fear of what "might be" rather than focus on what is _real_ or true. Concentrate on what is true and positive.**

   Philippians 4:8 Finally, brothers, whatever is true, whatever is noble, whatever is right, whatever is pure, whatever is lovely, whatever is admirable—if anything is excellent or praiseworthy—think about such things.

4. **The bottom line is believing God is sufficient.**

   2 Corinthians 12:9–10 But he said to me, "My grace is sufficient for you, for my power is made perfect in weakness." Therefore I will boast all the more gladly about my weaknesses, so that Christ's power may rest on me. That is why, for Christ's sake, I delight in weaknesses, in insults, in hardships, in persecutions, in difficulties. For when I am weak, then I am strong.

5. **Do we believe God is sovereign? Our days are planned for our best. Trust puts anxiety to rest.**

   Psalm 139:16 Your eyes saw my unformed body. All the days ordained for me were written in your book before one of them came to be.

   Isaiah 44:6 This is what the LORD says—Israel's King and Redeemer, the LORD Almighty: I am the first and I am the last; apart from me there is no God.

   Isaiah 45:5–7 I am the LORD, and there is no other; apart from me there is no God. I will strengthen you, though you have not acknowledged me, so that from the rising of the sun to the place of its setting men may know there is none besides me. I am the LORD, and there is no other. I form the light and create darkness, I bring prosperity and create disaster; I, the LORD, do all these things.

6. **God can use anything for his ultimate plan. God wastes nothing.**

   Romans 8:28 And we know that in all things God works for the good of those who love him, who have been called according to his purpose.

7. **Anxiety for the future is cared for in God's ultimate plan.**

   John 14:1–3 Do not let your hearts be troubled. Trust in God; trust also in me. In my Father's house are many rooms; if it were not so, I would have told you. I am going there to prepare a place for you. And if I go and prepare a place for you, I will come back and take you to be with me that you also may be where I am.

Isaiah 26:3–4 You will keep in perfect peace him whose mind is steadfast, because he trusts in you. Trust in the LORD forever, for the LORD, the LORD, is the Rock eternal.

Matthew 6:33–34 But seek first his kingdom and his righteousness, and all these things will be given to you as well. Therefore do not worry about tomorrow, for tomorrow will worry about itself. Each day has enough trouble of its own.

Birth Control

Scripture does not specifically speak to this issue; however, these principles apply.

1. **Children are gifts, blessings from God.**

   Psalm 127:3–5 Sons are a heritage from the LORD, children a reward from him. Like arrows in the hands of a warrior are sons born in one's youth. Blessed is the man whose quiver is full of them. They will not be put to shame when they contend with their enemies in the gate.

   Proverbs 17:6 Children's children are a crown to the aged, and parents are the pride of their children.

   Psalm 128:3–4 Your wife will be like a fruitful vine within your house; your sons will be like olive shoots around your table. Thus is the man blessed who fears the LORD.

   Matthew 18:5 And whoever welcomes a little child like this in my name welcomes me.

2. **Decisions need to be made prayerfully, seeking God's wisdom for guidance.**

   James 1:5 If any of you lacks wisdom, he should ask God, who gives generously to all without finding fault, and it will be given to him.

Ephesians 5:15–17 Be very careful, then, how you live—not as unwise but as wise, making the most of every opportunity, because the days are evil. Therefore do not be foolish, but understand what the Lord's will is.

Psalm 32:8 I will instruct you and teach you in the way you should go; I will counsel you and watch over you.

Proverbs 3:5–6 Trust in the LORD with all your heart and lean not on your own understanding; in all your ways acknowledge him, and he will make your paths straight.

Proverbs 2:6–7 For the LORD gives wisdom, and from his mouth come knowledge and understanding. He holds victory in store for the upright, he is a shield to those whose walk is blameless.

James 3:17 But the wisdom that comes from heaven is first of all pure; then peace-loving, considerate, submissive, full of mercy and good fruit, impartial and sincere.

3. God is sovereign; he will accomplish what he wants to accomplish.

Job 42:2 I know that you can do all things; no plan of yours can be thwarted.

Ephesians 1:11 In him we were also chosen, having been predestined according to the plan of him who works out everything in conformity with the purpose of his will.

Bitterness

1. **Bitterness grows, causes trouble, and affects others.**

   Hebrews 12:15 See to it that no one misses the grace of God and that no bitter root grows up to cause trouble and defile many.

   James 3:14–16 But if you harbor bitter envy and selfish ambition in your hearts, do not boast about it or deny the truth. Such "wisdom" does not come down from heaven but is earthly, unspiritual, of the devil. For where you have envy and selfish ambition, there you find disorder and every evil practice.

2. **Bitterness is not something to retain.**

   Ephesians 4:31–32 Get rid of all bitterness, rage and anger, brawling and slander, along with every form of malice. Be kind and compassionate to one another, forgiving each other, just as in Christ God forgave you.

3. **Each person has his own areas of bitterness with which to contend.**

   Proverbs 14:10 Each heart knows its own bitterness, and no one else can share its joy.

4. **Bitterness is a mark of the unsaved.**

   Romans 3:14 Their mouths are full of cursing and bitterness.

Broken Heart

1. **Those who have a broken heart are dear to God's heart.**

   Psalm 34:18 The LORD is close to the brokenhearted and saves those who are crushed in spirit.

   Psalm 147:3 He heals the brokenhearted and binds up their wounds.

2. **God can make sense out of the senseless.**

   Jeremiah 33:3 Call to me and I will answer you and tell you great and unsearchable things you do not know.

3. **For whatever reason there is a broken heart, God in his sovereignty comforts us, and that teaches us how to help those who are hurting.**

   2 Corinthians 1:3–4 Praise be to the God and Father of our Lord Jesus Christ, the Father of compassion and the God of all comfort, who comforts us in all our troubles, so that we can comfort those in any trouble with the comfort we ourselves have received from God.

4. **A broken heart can draw one close to God.**

   Psalm 51:17 The sacrifices of God are a broken spirit; a broken and contrite heart, O God, you will not despise.

   John 14:1 Jesus said, "Do not let your hearts be troubled. Trust in God; trust also in me."

Career/
Working outside the Home

See also Mothering, God's Will

1. **A mother's first and foremost responsibility needs to be caring for her home and her children.**

   Proverbs 14:1 The wise woman builds her house, but with her own hands the foolish one tears hers down.

   Titus 2:3–5 Likewise, teach the older women to be reverent in the way they live, not to be slanderers or addicted to much wine, but to teach what is good. Then they can train the younger women to love their husbands and children, to be self-controlled and pure, to be busy at home, to be kind, and to be subject to their husbands, so that no one will malign the word of God.

   1 Timothy 5:14 So I counsel younger widows to marry, to have children, to manage their homes and to give the enemy no opportunity for slander.

   For further reference see Proverbs 31:10–31.

2. **Children need what a mother can give.**

   Isaiah 49:15 Can a mother forget the baby at her breast and have no compassion on the child she has borne? Though she may forget, I will not forget you!

Proverbs 19:18 Discipline your son, for in that there is hope; do not be a willing party to his death.

Proverbs 31:28 Her children arise and call her blessed; her husband also, and he praises her.

Isaiah 66:13 As a mother comforts her child, so will I comfort you; and you will be comforted over Jerusalem.

Deuteronomy 6:4–9 Hear, O Israel: The LORD our God, the LORD is one. Love the LORD your God with all your heart and with all your soul and with all your strength. These commandments that I give you today are to be upon your hearts. Impress them on your children. Talk about them when you sit at home and when you walk along the road, when you lie down and when you get up. Tie them as symbols on your hands and bind them on your foreheads. Write them on the doorframes of your houses and on your gates.

3. **The capable mother in Proverbs 31 was involved in business; however, her home did not suffer.**

   Proverbs 31:14–18, 24 She is like the merchant ships, bringing her food from afar. She gets up while it is still dark; she provides food for her family and portions for her servant girls. She considers a field and buys it; out of her earnings she plants a vineyard. She sets about her work vigorously; her arms are strong for her tasks. She sees that her trading is profitable, and her lamp does not go out at night. . . . She makes linen garments and sells them, and supplies the merchants with sashes.

4. **When involved in both business and home, business can never take over the primary responsibility of home. Balance is crucial.**

   Ecclesiastes 7:18 It is good to grasp the one and not let go of the other. The man who fears God will avoid all *extremes*.

Care of Elderly Parents/In-Laws

1. **Honor is not given an age limit.**

   Exodus 20:12 Honor your father and your mother, so that you may live long in the land the LORD your God is giving you.

2. **Live at peace with everyone, in-laws and parents included.**

   Romans 12:18 If it is possible, as far as it depends on you, live at peace with everyone.

3. **It is our responsibility in some way to provide care for our family members.**

   1 Timothy 5:8 If anyone does not provide for his relatives, and especially for his immediate family, he has denied the faith and is worse than an unbeliever.

   Philippians 2:14 Do everything without complaining or arguing.

4. **God gives significance to old age; should we not also?**

   Isaiah 46:4 Even to your old age and gray hairs I am he, I am he who will sustain you. I have made you and I will carry you; I will sustain you and I will rescue you.

5. **The blessing of old age.**

   Psalm 128:6 And may you live to see your children's children.

Co-dependency

See also Self-Worth

1. **Our ultimate dependency needs to be on God alone.**

   Psalm 62:7–8 My salvation and my honor depend on God; he is my mighty rock, my refuge. Trust in him at all times, O people; pour out your hearts to him, for God is our refuge.

   Jeremiah 17:5 This is what the LORD says: "Cursed is the one who trusts in man, who depends on flesh for his strength and whose heart turns away from the LORD."

   Psalm 20:7–8 Some trust in chariots and some in horses, but we trust in the name of the LORD our God. They are brought to their knees and fall, but we rise up and stand firm.

   Zechariah 4:6 "Not by might nor by power, but by my Spirit," says the LORD Almighty.

   We have access to God

   Hebrews 4:16 Let us then approach the throne of grace with confidence, so that we may receive mercy and find grace to help us in our time of need.

   God does not change

   Malachi 3:6a I the LORD do not change.

2. **The Israelites met failure by depending on self; we should not depend on self.**

   Hosea 10:13 But you have planted wickedness, you have reaped evil, you have eaten the fruit of deception. Because you have depended on your own strength and on your many warriors . . .

3. **Depending on self is foolish.**

   Proverbs 28:26 He who trusts in himself is a fool, but he who walks in wisdom is kept safe.

   2 Corinthians 1:9 Indeed, in our hearts we felt the sentence of death. But this happened that we might not rely on ourselves but on God, who raises the dead.

4. **A positive goal is not to be dependent on others in an unhealthy way.**

   1 Thessalonians 4:11–12 Make it your ambition to lead a quiet life, to mind your own business and to work with your hands, just as we told you, so that your daily life may win the respect of outsiders and so that you will not be dependent on anybody.

5. **The biblical view is a healthy interdependence between husband and wife.**

   1 Corinthians 11:11 In the Lord, however, woman is not independent of man, nor is man independent of woman.

6. **The biblical view is a healthy balance between trusting and doing.**

Nehemiah's Example

Nehemiah 4:8–9 They all plotted together to come and fight against Jerusalem and stir up trouble against it. But we prayed to our God and posted a guard day and night to meet this threat.

Communication/Speech

See also Lying, Gossip

1. **Positive qualities to develop in speech.**

   Edification (building up of others)

   Ephesians 4:29 Do not let any unwholesome talk come out of your mouths, but only what is helpful for building others up according to their needs, that it may benefit those who listen.

   Gentleness

   Proverbs 25:15 Through patience a ruler can be persuaded, and a gentle tongue can break a bone.

Speaking truth

Ephesians 4:25 Therefore each of you must put off falsehood and speak truthfully to his neighbor, for we are all members of one body.

Slow to speak

James 1:19–20 My dear brothers, take note of this: Everyone should be quick to listen, slow to speak and slow to become angry, for man's anger does not bring about the righteous life that God desires.

Proverbs 15:28 The heart of the righteous weighs its answers, but the mouth of the wicked gushes evil.

Speaking knowledge

Proverbs 20:15 Gold there is, and rubies in abundance, but lips that speak knowledge are a rare jewel.

Appropriate words

Proverbs 25:11 A word aptly spoken is like apples of gold in settings of silver.

Proverbs 15:23 A man finds joy in giving an apt reply—and how good is a timely word!

Kindness

Proverbs 12:25 An anxious heart weighs a man down, but a kind word cheers him up.

2. Negative qualities to avoid in speech.

Obscene, foolish, raw jokes

Ephesians 5:4 Nor should there be obscenity, foolish talk or coarse joking, which are out of place, but rather thanksgiving.

Ephesians 4:29 Do not let any unwholesome talk come out of your mouths, but only what is helpful for building others up according to their needs, that it may benefit those who listen.

Falsehood, lying

Ephesians 4:25 Therefore each of you must put off falsehood and speak truthfully to his neighbor.

Answering before listening

Proverbs 18:13 He who answers before listening—that is his folly and his shame.

Foolish, stupid arguments

2 Timothy 2:23–24 Don't have anything to do with foolish and stupid arguments, because you know they produce quarrels. And the Lord's servant must not quarrel; instead, he must be kind to everyone, able to teach, not resentful.

Slander

Titus 3:1–2 Remind the people to be subject to rulers and authorities, to be obedient, to be ready to do whatever is good, to slander no one, to be peaceable and considerate, and to show true humility toward all men.

Ephesians 4:31 Get rid of all bitterness, rage and anger, brawling and slander, along with every form of malice.

Lack of control

James 1:26 If anyone considers himself religious and yet does not keep a tight rein on his tongue, he deceives himself and his religion is worthless.

3. **Speech can both grieve and please the Holy Spirit.**

Ephesians 4:29–30 Do not let any unwholesome talk come out of your mouths, but only what is helpful for building others up according to their needs, that it may benefit those who listen. And do not grieve the Holy Spirit of God, with whom you were sealed for the day of redemption.

4. **Summary of the tongue's power potential.**

James 3:5–10 Likewise the tongue is a small part of the body, but it makes great boasts. Consider what a great forest is set on fire by a small spark. The tongue also is a fire, a world of evil among the parts of the body. It corrupts the whole person, sets the whole course of his life on fire, and is itself set on fire by hell. All kinds of animals, birds, reptiles and creatures of the sea are being tamed and have been tamed by man, but no man can tame the tongue. It is a restless evil, full of deadly poison. With the tongue we praise our Lord and Father, and with it we curse men, who have been made in God's likeness. Out of the same mouth come praise and cursing. My brothers, this should not be.

Confession/Repentance

See also Guilt, Forgiveness

1. **Without confession/repentance there is no freedom.**

   Isaiah 38:17 Surely it was for my benefit that I suffered such anguish. In your love you kept me from the pit of destruction; you have put all my sins behind your back.

2. **Confession for sin is God's desire.**

   Ezra 10:11 Now make confession to the LORD, the God of your fathers, and do his will.

   1 John 1:9 If we confess our sins, he is faithful and just and will forgive us our sins and purify us from all unrighteousness.

   Psalm 66:18 If I had cherished sin in my heart, the Lord would not have listened.

3. **Confession leads to healing.**

   Proverbs 28:13 He who conceals his sins does not prosper, but whoever confesses and renounces them finds mercy.

4. **Confession of Jesus as Savior leads to rejoicing.**

   Luke 15:10 In the same way, I tell you, there is rejoicing in the presence of the angels of God over one sinner who repents.

   Romans 10:9 That if you confess with your mouth, "Jesus is Lord," and believe in your heart that God raised him from the dead, you will be saved.

Contentment

1. **Contentment is trusting God no matter what the circumstances.**

   Psalm 16:6 The boundary lines have fallen for me in pleasant places; surely I have a delightful inheritance.

   Exodus 33:14 The LORD replied, "My Presence will go with you, and I will give you rest."

   Isaiah 26:3 You will keep in perfect peace him whose mind is steadfast, because he trusts in you.

   Psalm 37:7, 16 Be still before the LORD and wait patiently for him; do not fret when men succeed in their ways, when they carry out their wicked schemes. . . .Better the little that the righteous have than the wealth of many wicked.

   Psalm 118:24 This is the day the LORD has made; let us rejoice and be glad in it.

2. **Contentment in material possessions.**

   Hebrews 13:5 Keep your lives free from the love of money and be content with what you have, because God has said, "Never will I leave you; never will I forsake you."

   1 Timothy 6:6–8 But godliness with contentment is great gain. For we brought nothing into the world, and we can take nothing out of it. But if we have food and clothing, we will be content with that.

Proverbs 16:8 Better a little with righteousness than much gain with injustice.

Proverbs 17:1 Better a dry crust with peace and quiet than a house full of feasting, with strife.

Ecclesiastes 2:24 A man can do nothing better than to eat and drink and find satisfaction in his work. This too, I see, is from the hand of God.

Philippians 4:11–12 I am not saying this because I am in need, for I have learned to be content whatever the circumstances. I know what it is to be in need, and I know what it is to have plenty. I have learned the secret of being content in any and every situation, whether well fed or hungry, whether living in plenty or in want.

Dating/Courtship

See also Sexual Purity, God's Will, Singleness

1. In biblical times obtaining a mate involved parental arranging for a marriage or wives obtained by purchase or reward.
2. Today customs involve the young adult in the decision.

Considerations:

1. Yielding to God's will as part of the decision.

   Psalm 37:3–4 Trust in the LORD and do good; dwell in the land and enjoy safe pasture. Delight yourself in the LORD and he will give you the desires of your heart.

   Ecclesiastes 12:1 Remember your Creator in the days of your youth, before the days of trouble come and the years approach when you will say, "I find no pleasure in them."

2. It is good to have parental involvement and support in this area as well as others.

   Proverbs 6:20–25 My son, keep your father's commands and do not forsake your mother's teaching. Bind them upon your heart forever; fasten them around your neck. When you walk, they will guide you; when you sleep, they will watch over you; when you awake, they will speak to you. For these commands are a lamp, this teaching is a light, and the corrections of discipline are the way to life, keeping you from the immoral woman, from the smooth tongue of the wayward wife. Do not lust in your heart after her beauty or let her captivate you with her eyes.

Proverbs 1:8–9 Listen, my son, to your father's instruction and do not forsake your mother's teaching. They will be a garland to grace your head and a chain to adorn your neck.

Proverbs 5:1–2 My son, pay attention to my wisdom, listen well to my words of insight, that you may maintain discretion and your lips may preserve knowledge.

3. **Dating/courtship for marriage should only be with another believer.**

   2 Corinthians 6:14 Do not be yoked together with unbelievers. For what do righteousness and wickedness have in common? Or what fellowship can light have with darkness?

4. **Standards and guidelines need to be in place with an understanding of sexual purity.**

   Job 31:1 I made a covenant with my eyes not to look lustfully at a girl.

   1 Timothy 4:12 Don't let anyone look down on you because you are young, but set an example for the believers in speech, in life, in love, in faith and in purity.

   2 Timothy 2:22 Flee the evil desires of youth, and pursue righteousness, faith, love and peace, along with those who call on the Lord out of a pure heart.

   1 Thessalonians 4:3–4 It is God's will that you should be sanctified: that you should avoid sexual immorality; that each of you should learn to control his own body in a way that is holy and honorable.

Death/Grief

Fear of Death

1. **Death does not separate us from God and his love.**

   Psalm 23:4 Even though I walk through the valley of the shadow of death, I will fear no evil, for you are with me; your rod and your staff, they comfort me.

   Psalm 116:15 Precious in the sight of the LORD is the death of his saints.

   Romans 8:38–39 For I am convinced that neither death nor life, neither angels nor demons, neither the present nor the future, nor any powers, neither height nor depth, nor anything else in all creation, will be able to separate us from the love of God that is in Christ Jesus our Lord.

2. **Death for the believer means being in the presence of Christ.**

   Philippians 1:21–23 For to me, to live is Christ and to die is gain. If I am to go on living in the body, this will mean fruitful labor for me. Yet what shall I choose? I do not know! I am torn between the two: I desire to depart and be with Christ, which is better by far . . .

   2 Corinthians 5:6–8 Therefore we are always confident and know that as long as we are at home in the body we are away from the Lord. We live by faith, not by sight. We are confident, I say, and would prefer to be away from the body and at home with the Lord.

3. **Death for a believer means receiving a new and glorious body.**

Philippians 3:21 Who, by the power that enables him to bring everything under his control, will transform our lowly bodies so that they will be like his glorious body.

1 Corinthians 15:52 In a flash, in the twinkling of an eye, at the last trumpet. For the trumpet will sound, the dead will be raised imperishable, and we will be changed.

1 John 3:2 Dear friends, now we are children of God, and what we will be has not yet been made known. But we know that when he appears, we shall be like him, for we shall see him as he is.

4. **Jesus' death gives ultimate freedom from fear.**

Hebrews 2:9–15 But we see Jesus, who was made a little lower than the angels, now crowned with glory and honor because he suffered death, so that by the grace of God he might taste death for everyone. In bringing many sons to glory, it was fitting that God, for whom and through whom everything exists, should make the author of their salvation perfect through suffering. Both the one who makes men holy and those who are made holy are of the same family. So Jesus is not ashamed to call them brothers. He says, "I will declare your name to my brothers; in the presence of the congregation I will sing your praises." And again, "I will put my trust in him." And again he says, "Here am I, and the children God has given me." Since the children have flesh and blood, he too shared in their humanity so that by his death he might destroy him who holds the power of death—that is, the devil—and free those who all their lives were held in slavery by their fear of death.

5. **God's strength is always available.**

Deuteronomy 31:6 Be strong and courageous. Do not be afraid or terrified because of them, for the LORD your God goes with you; he will never leave you nor forsake you.

Isaiah 26:3 You will keep in perfect peace him whose mind is steadfast, because he trusts in you.

Isaiah 41:10 So do not fear, for I am with you; do not be dismayed, for I am your God. I will strengthen you and help you; I will uphold you with my righteous right hand.

Lamentations 3:21–24 Yet this I call to mind and therefore I have hope: Because of the LORD's great love we are not consumed, for his compassions never fail. They are new every morning; great is your faithfulness. I say to myself, "The LORD is my portion; therefore I will wait for him."

Loss by Death

1. **David expresses his grief to God.**

   Psalm 31:9–10 Be merciful to me, O LORD, for I am in distress; my eyes grow weak with sorrow, my soul and my body with grief. My life is consumed by anguish and my years by groaning; my strength fails because of my affliction, and my bones grow weak.

2. **God cares for and understands the broken heart.**

   Psalm 147:3 He heals the brokenhearted and binds up their wounds.

   John 14:1 Do not let your hearts be troubled. Trust in God; trust also in me.

3. **There is hope for the future after death.**

   1 Corinthians 15:51–52 Listen, I tell you a mystery: We will not all sleep, but we will all be changed—in a flash, in the twinkling of an eye, at the last trumpet. For the trumpet will sound, the dead will be raised imperishable, and we will be changed.

4. **God can restore joy.**

   Isaiah 51:11 The ransomed of the LORD will return. They will enter Zion with singing; everlasting joy will crown their heads. Gladness and joy will overtake them, and sorrow and sighing will flee away.

Depression

1. **Depression is a heavy burden and feels insurmountable.**

   Proverbs 18:14 A man's spirit sustains him in sickness, but a crushed spirit who can bear?

   Psalm 69:1–2 Save me, O God, for the waters have come up to my neck. I sink in the miry depths, where there is no foothold. I have come into the deep waters; the floods engulf me.

2. **Is sin involved in this depression? Cain was depressed because of sin in his life.**

   Genesis 4:6–7 Then the LORD said to Cain, "Why are you angry? Why is your face downcast? If you do what is right, will you not be accepted? But if you do not do what is right, sin is crouching at your door; it desires to have you, but you must master it."

3. **When sin is the cause of depression, step one is confession to God as David did after his sin.**

   Psalm 51:1–18 Have mercy on me, O God, according to your unfailing love; according to your great compassion blot out my transgressions. Wash away all my iniquity and cleanse me from my sin. For I know my transgressions, and my sin is always before me. Against you, you only, have I sinned and done what is evil in your sight, so that you are proved right when you speak and justified when you judge. Surely I was sinful at birth, sinful from the time my mother conceived me. Surely you desire truth in the inner parts; you teach me wisdom in the inmost place. Cleanse me with hyssop, and I will be clean; wash me, and I will be whiter than snow. Let me hear joy and gladness; let the bones you have crushed rejoice. Hide your face from my sins and blot out all my iniquity. Create in me a pure heart, O God, and renew a steadfast spirit within me. Do not cast me from your presence or take your Holy Spirit from me. Restore to me the joy of your salvation and grant me a willing spirit, to sustain me. Then I will teach transgressors your ways, and sinners will turn back to you. Save me from bloodguilt, O God, the God who saves me, and my tongue will sing of your righteousness. O Lord, open my lips, and my mouth will declare your praise. You do not delight in sacrifice, or I would bring it; you do not take pleasure in burnt offerings. The sacrifices of God are a broken spirit; a broken and contrite heart, O God, you will not despise. In your good pleasure make Zion prosper; build up the walls of Jerusalem.

Psalm 32:3–8 When I kept silent, my bones wasted away through my groaning all day long. For day and night your hand was heavy upon me; my strength was sapped as in the heat of summer. Then I acknowledged my sin to you and did not cover up my iniquity. I said, "I will confess my transgressions to the LORD"—and you forgave the guilt of my sin. Therefore let everyone who is godly pray to you while you may be found; surely when the mighty waters rise, they will not reach him. You are my hiding place; you will protect me from trouble and surround me with songs of deliverance. I will instruct you and teach you in the way you should go; I will counsel you and watch over you.

4. **God is the answer to a life in despair.**

    Psalm 43:5 Why are you downcast, O my soul? Why so disturbed within me? Put your hope in God, for I will yet praise him, my Savior and my God.

    Psalm 46:1 God is our refuge and strength, an ever-present help in trouble.

    2 Corinthians 4:16 Therefore we do not lose heart. Though outwardly we are wasting away, yet inwardly we are being renewed day by day.

5. **God understands despair.**

   Psalm 18:28 You, O LORD, keep my lamp burning; my God turns my darkness into light.

   Psalm 38:9 All my longings lie open before you, O Lord; my sighing is not hidden from you.

   Job 23:10 But he knows the way that I take; when he has tested me, I will come forth as gold.

6. **There is hope in God.**

   Psalm 16:8 I have set the LORD always before me. Because he is at my right hand, I will not be shaken.

   Hebrews 12:2 Let us fix our eyes on Jesus, the author and perfecter of our faith, who for the joy set before him endured the cross, scorning its shame, and sat down at the right hand of the throne of God.

   Ephesians 1:17–19 I keep asking that the God of our Lord Jesus Christ, the glorious Father, may give you the Spirit of wisdom and revelation, so that you may know him better. I pray also that the eyes of your heart may be enlightened in order that you may know the hope to which he has called you, the riches of his glorious inheritance in the saints, and his incomparably great power for us who believe.

NOTE: It would be beneficial to have the counselee see a physician to eliminate the possibility of physiological causes.

Discipleship/Mentoring

1. **Mandate for mentoring.**

   2 Timothy 2:1–2 You then, my son, be strong in the grace that is in Christ Jesus. And the things you have heard me say in the presence of many witnesses entrust to reliable men who will also be qualified to teach others.

   Matthew 28:19–20 Therefore go and make disciples of all nations, baptizing them in the name of the Father and of the Son and of the Holy Spirit, and teaching them to obey everything I have commanded you. And surely I am with you always, to the very end of the age.

   Colossians 1:28 We proclaim him, admonishing and teaching everyone with all wisdom, so that we may present everyone perfect in Christ.

2. **Ingredients for mentoring.**

   Titus 2:3–5 Likewise, teach the older women to be reverent in the way they live, not to be slanderers or addicted to much wine, but to teach what is good. Then they can train the younger women to love their husbands and children, to be self-controlled and pure, to be busy at home, to be kind, and to be subject to their husbands, so that no one will malign the word of God.

3. Qualities of those who mentor.

Believers, prepared, gentle, respectful

1 Peter 3:15 But in your hearts set apart Christ as Lord. Always be prepared to give an answer to everyone who asks you to give the reason for the hope that you have. But do this with gentleness and respect.

Encouragers

Isaiah 35:3–4 Strengthen the feeble hands, steady the knees that give way; say to those with fearful hearts, "Be strong, do not fear; your God will come, he will come with vengeance; with divine retribution he will come to save you."

Hebrews 12:12–13 Therefore, strengthen your feeble arms and weak knees. "Make level paths for your feet," so that the lame may not be disabled, but rather healed.

Communicators

Proverbs 20:5 The purposes of a man's heart are deep waters, but a man of understanding draws them out.

Prayerful

John 17:9 I pray for them. I am not praying for the world, but for those you have given me, for they are yours.

Self-sacrificing

2 Corinthians 12:15 So I will very gladly spend for you everything I have and expend myself as well. If I love you more, will you love me less?

Disciplining Children

See also Training Children, Mothering

1. **God disciplines in love—parents should also discipline in love.**

   Hebrews 12:5–11 "My son, do not make light of the Lord's discipline, and do not lose heart when he rebukes you, because the Lord disciplines those he loves, and he punishes everyone he accepts as a son." Endure hardship as discipline; God is treating you as sons. For what son is not disciplined by his father? If you are not disciplined (and everyone undergoes discipline), then you are illegitimate children and not true sons. Moreover, we have all had human fathers who disciplined us and we respected them for it. How much more should we submit to the Father of our spirits and live! Our fathers disciplined us for a little while as they thought best; but God disciplines us for our good, that we may share in his holiness No discipline seems pleasant at the time, but painful. Later on, however, it produces a harvest of righteousness and peace for those who have been trained by it.

   Proverbs 13:24 He who spares the rod hates his son, but he who loves him is careful to discipline him.

   Psalm 103:13 As a father has compassion on his children, so the LORD has compassion on those who fear him.

2. **Without discipline there cannot be successful maturity.**

   Proverbs 19:18 Discipline your son, for in that there is hope; do not be a willing party to his death.

   Proverbs 29:15 The rod of correction imparts wisdom, but a child left to himself disgraces his mother.

   Proverbs 19:20 Listen to advice and accept instruction, and in the end you will be wise.

   Proverbs 22:6 Train a child in the way he should go, and when he is old he will not turn from it.

   Proverbs 15:31–32 He who listens to a life-giving rebuke will be at home among the wise. He who ignores discipline despises himself, but whoever heeds correction gains understanding.

3. **Parents are not to push children to frustration.**

   Ephesians 6:4 Fathers, do not exasperate your children; instead, bring them up in the training and instruction of the Lord.

   Colossians 3:21 Fathers, do not embitter your children, or they will become discouraged.

4. **Physical punishment is acceptable but needs to be done in love and without extreme.**

   Proverbs 23:13–14 Do not withhold discipline from a child; if you punish him with the rod, he will not die. Punish him with the rod and save his soul from death.

   Proverbs 22:15 Folly is bound up in the heart of a child, but the rod of discipline will drive it far from him.

Divorce

See also Marriage

1. **God created marriage to be lasting.**

    Matthew 19:6 So they are no longer two, but one. Therefore what God has joined together, let man not separate.

    1 Corinthians 7:39 A woman is bound to her husband as long as he lives. But if her husband dies, she is free to marry anyone she wishes, but he must belong to the Lord.

2. **God's choice is not divorce.**

    Malachi 2:15–16 Has not the LORD made them one? In flesh and spirit they are his. And why one? Because he was seeking godly offspring. So guard yourself in your spirit, and do not break faith with the wife of your youth. "I hate divorce," says the LORD God of Israel, "and I hate a man's covering himself with violence as well as with his garment," says the LORD Almighty. So guard yourself in your spirit, and do not break faith.

    1 Corinthians 7:10–11 To the married I give this command (not I, but the Lord): A wife must not separate from her husband. But if she does, she must remain unmarried or else be reconciled to her husband. And a husband must not divorce his wife.

Luke 16:18 Anyone who divorces his wife and marries another woman commits adultery, and the man who marries a divorced woman commits adultery.

3. **God permitted divorce because of the hardness of Israel's heart.**

Matthew 19:3–8 Some Pharisees came to him to test him. They asked, "Is it lawful for a man to divorce his wife for any and every reason?" "Haven't you read," he replied, "that at the beginning the Creator 'made them male and female,' and said, 'For this reason a man will leave his father and mother and be united to his wife, and the two will become one flesh'? So they are no longer two, but one. Therefore what God has joined together, let man not separate." "Why then," they asked, "did Moses command that a man give his wife a certificate of divorce and send her away?" Jesus replied, "Moses permitted you to divorce your wives because your hearts were hard. But it was not this way from the beginning."

Mark 10:3–5 "What did Moses command you?" he replied. They said, "Moses permitted a man to write a certificate of divorce and send her away." "It was because your hearts were hard that Moses wrote you this law," Jesus replied.

4. **God permits divorce because of unfaithfulness.**

Matthew 5:31–32 It has been said, 'Anyone who divorces his wife must give her a certificate of divorce.' But I tell you that anyone who divorces his wife, except for marital unfaithfulness, causes her to become an adulteress, and anyone who marries the divorced woman commits adultery.

5. **Because a mate is not a believer is not a reason for divorce.**

1 Corinthians 7:12–17 To the rest I say this (I, not the Lord): If any brother has a wife who is not a believer and she is willing to live with him, he must not divorce her. And if a woman has a husband who is not a believer and he is willing to live with her, she must not divorce him. For the unbelieving husband has been sanctified through his wife, and the unbelieving wife has been sanctified through her believing husband. Otherwise your children would be unclean, but as it is, they are holy. But if the unbeliever leaves, let him do so.

A believing man or woman is not bound in such circumstances; God has called us to live in peace. How do you know, wife, whether you will save your husband? Or, how do you know, husband, whether you will save your wife? Nevertheless, each one should retain the place in life that the Lord assigned to him and to which God has called him. This is the rule I lay down in all the churches.

Eating Disorders

1. **Our trust, success, and security is not in our bodies, but in God.**

   Jeremiah 17:5–7 This is what the LORD says: "Cursed is the one who trusts in man, who depends on flesh for his strength and whose heart turns away from the LORD. He will be like a bush in the wastelands; he will not see prosperity when it comes. He will dwell in the parched places of the desert, in a salt land where no one lives. But blessed is the man who trusts in the LORD, whose confidence is in him."

   Zechariah 4:6 "Not by might nor by power, but by my Spirit," says the LORD Almighty.

   Philippians 3:7–9 But whatever was to my profit I now consider loss for the sake of Christ. What is more, I consider everything a loss compared to the surpassing greatness of knowing Christ Jesus my Lord, for whose sake I have lost all things. I consider them rubbish, that I may gain Christ and be found in him, not having a righteousness of my own that comes from the law, but that which is through faith in Christ—the righteousness that comes from God and is by faith.

2. **Taking control of what belongs to God is sin. Focusing on self is idolatry.**

   Colossians 3:5 Put to death, therefore, whatever belongs to your earthly nature: sexual immorality, impurity, lust, evil desires and greed, which is idolatry.

   Psalm 103:2–3, 12–13 Praise the LORD, O my soul, and forget not all his benefits—who forgives all your sins and heals all your diseases . . . as far as the east is from the west, so far has he removed our transgressions from us. As a father has compassion on his children, so the LORD has compassion on those who fear him.

   1 John 1:8–9 If we claim to be without sin, we deceive ourselves and the truth is not in us. If we confess our sins, he is faithful and just and will forgive us our sins and purify us from all unrighteousness.

3. **The body belongs to God.**

   1 Corinthians 3:16–17 Don't you know that you yourselves are God's temple and that God's Spirit lives in you? If anyone destroys God's temple, God will destroy him; for God's temple is sacred, and you are that temple.

   1 Corinthians 6:19–20 Do you not know that your body is a temple of the Holy Spirit, who is in you, whom you have received from God? You are not your own; you were bought at a price. Therefore honor God with your body.

4. **By an act of the will we are to give our bodies back to God.**

   Romans 12:1–2 Therefore, I urge you, brothers, in view of God's mercy, to offer your bodies as living sacrifices, holy and pleasing to God—this is your spiritual act of worship. Do not conform any longer to the pattern of this world, but be transformed by the renewing of your mind. Then you will be able to test and approve what God's will is—his good, pleasing and perfect will.

5. **Changing thinking is crucial.**

   Isaiah 55:8–9 "For my thoughts are not your thoughts, neither are your ways my ways," declares the LORD. "As the heavens are higher than the earth, so are my ways higher than your ways and my thoughts than your thoughts."

Philippians 4:8–9 Finally, brothers, whatever is true, whatever is noble, whatever is right, whatever is pure, whatever is lovely, whatever is admirable—if anything is excellent or praiseworthy— think about such things. Whatever you have learned or received or heard from me, or seen in me—put it into practice. And the God of peace will be with you.

6. **Pray before eating and give thanks, for what God has created is good.**

1 Timothy 4:4–5 For everything God created is good, and nothing is to be rejected if it is received with thanksgiving, because it is consecrated by the word of God and prayer.

1 Timothy 6:17 Command those who are rich in this present world not to be arrogant nor to put their hope in wealth, which is so uncertain, but to put their hope in God, who richly provides us with everything for our enjoyment.

Ephesians 5:29 After all, no one ever hated his own body, but he feeds and cares for it, just as Christ does the church.

NOTE: It would be beneficial to have the counselee see a physician.

Empty Nest

1. **The goal of raising children is to have them leave home as mature, God-fearing adults, ready to have their own homes.**

   Genesis 2:24 For this reason a man will leave his father and mother and be united to his wife, and they will become one flesh.

   Proverbs 17:6 Children's children are a crown to the aged, and parents are the pride of their children.

   Psalm 78:5–6 He decreed statutes for Jacob and established the law in Israel, which he commanded our forefathers to teach their children, so the next generation would know them, even the children yet to be born, and they in turn would tell their children.

   Joel 1:3 Tell it to your children, and let your children tell it to their children, and their children to the next generation.

2. **Use this time to focus on your mate.**

   Proverbs 21:19 Better to live in a desert than with a quarrelsome and ill-tempered wife.

   Hebrews 3:4 For every house is built by someone, but God is the builder of everything.

   1 Corinthians 7:3–5 The husband should fulfill his marital duty to his wife, and likewise the wife to her husband. The wife's body does not belong to her alone but also to her husband. In the same way, the husband's body does not belong to him alone but also to his wife. Do not deprive each other except by mutual consent and for a time, so that you may devote yourselves to prayer. Then come together again so that Satan will not tempt you because of your lack of self-control.

Proverbs 5:18 May your fountain be blessed, and may you rejoice in the wife of your youth.

3. **Focus on ministry as time is more free.**

Titus 2:3–5 Likewise, teach the older women to be reverent in the way they live, not to be slanderers or addicted to much wine, but to teach what is good. Then they can train the younger women to love their husbands and children, to be self-controlled and pure, to be busy at home, to be kind, and to be subject to their husbands, so that no one will malign the word of God.

Psalm 92:12–14 The righteous will flourish like a palm tree, they will grow like a cedar of Lebanon; planted in the house of the LORD, they will flourish in the courts of our God. They will still bear fruit in old age, they will stay fresh and green.

Anna's Example

Luke 2:36–37 There was also a prophetess, Anna, the daughter of Phanuel, of the tribe of Asher. She was very old; she had lived with her husband seven years after her marriage, and then was a widow until she was eighty-four. She never left the temple but worshiped night and day, fasting and praying.

4. **God provides for us as we age.**

Isaiah 46:4 Even to your old age and gray hairs I am he, I am he who will sustain you. I have made you and I will carry you; I will sustain you and I will rescue you.

Psalm 55:22 Cast your cares on the LORD and he will sustain you; he will never let the righteous fall.

Philippians 4:6–7 Do not be anxious about anything, but in everything, by prayer and petition, with thanksgiving, present your requests to God. And the peace of God, which transcends all understanding, will guard your hearts and your minds in Christ Jesus.

Fantasizing

See also Lust

1. **We must have right thinking.**

    Philippians 4:8 Finally, brothers, whatever is true, whatever is noble, whatever is right, whatever is pure, whatever is lovely, whatever is admirable—if anything is excellent or praiseworthy—think about such things.

2. **No place or thought is hidden from God.**

    Jeremiah 23:23–24 "Am I only a God nearby," declares the LORD, "and not a God far away? Can anyone hide in secret places so that I cannot see him?" declares the LORD. "Do not I fill heaven and earth?" declares the LORD.

3. **When God's thoughts and our thoughts do not match, we need to change our thinking.**

    Ephesians 4:22–24 You were taught, with regard to your former way of life, to put off your old self, which is being corrupted by its deceitful desires; to be made new in the attitude of your minds; and to put on the new self, created to be like God in true righteousness and holiness.

    Hebrews 12:1 Therefore, since we are surrounded by such a great cloud of witnesses, let us throw off everything that hinders and the sin that so easily entangles, and let us run with perseverance the race marked out for us.

4. Lustful thoughts are sinful and must be avoided.

Matthew 5:28 But I tell you that anyone who looks at a woman lustfully has already committed adultery with her in his heart.

1 Thessalonians 4:3–5 It is God's will that you should be sanctified: that you should avoid sexual immorality; that each of you should learn to control his own body in a way that is holy and honorable, not in passionate lust like the heathen, who do not know God.

Fear

See also Trust

1. **God is the answer to a fearful heart.**

   Psalm 34:4 I sought the LORD, and he answered me; he delivered me from all my fears.

   1 Peter 5:7 Cast all your anxiety on him because he cares for you.

2. **Do not focus on fear; focus on what is true or real.**

   Philippians 4:8 Finally, brothers, whatever is true, whatever is noble, whatever is right, whatever is pure, whatever is lovely, whatever is admirable—if anything is excellent or praiseworthy— think about such things.

3. **God is with us in every situation; therefore there is no need for fear.**

   Joshua 1:9 Have I not commanded you? Be strong and courageous. Do not be terrified; do not be discouraged, for the LORD your God will be with you wherever you go.

   Isaiah 41:10 So do not fear, for I am with you; do not be dismayed, for I am your God. I will strengthen you and help you; I will uphold you with my righteous right hand.

   Isaiah 41:13 For I am the LORD, your God, who takes hold of your right hand and says to you, Do not fear; I will help you.

Psalm 73:23–24 Yet I am always with you; you hold me by my right hand. You guide me with your counsel, and afterward you will take me into glory.

4. **If there is a fear problem, there is also a love problem.**

   1 John 4:18 There is no fear in love. But perfect love drives out fear, because fear has to do with punishment. The one who fears is not made perfect in love.

5. **Fear of the future.**

   Proverbs 3:5–6 Trust in the LORD with all your heart and lean not on your own understanding; in all your ways acknowledge him, and he will make your paths straight.

   Matthew 6:34 Therefore do not worry about tomorrow, for tomorrow will worry about itself. Each day has enough trouble of its own.

6. **Fear of not being provided for.**

   Matthew 6:26–33 Look at the birds of the air; they do not sow or reap or store away in barns, and yet your heavenly Father feeds them. Are you not much more valuable than they? Who of you by worrying can add a single hour to his life? And why do you worry about clothes? See how the lilies of the field grow. They do not labor or spin. Yet I tell you that not even Solomon in all his splendor was dressed like one of these. If that is how God clothes the grass of the field, which is here today and tomorrow is thrown into the fire, will he not much more clothe you, O you of little faith? So do not worry, saying, "What shall we eat?" or "What shall we drink?" or "What shall we wear?" For the pagans run after all these things, and your heavenly Father knows that you need them. But seek first his kingdom and his righteousness, and all these things will be given to you as well.

7. **Fear of the past.**

   Isaiah 43:18–19 Forget the former things; do not dwell on the past. See, I am doing a new thing! Now it springs up; do you not perceive it? I am making a way in the desert and streams in the wasteland.

8. **Fear of no protection.**

Psalm 91:4 He will cover you with his feathers, and under his wings you will find refuge; his faithfulness will be your shield and rampart.

Finances

1. **Part of what we earn needs to be given back to God.**

   Proverbs 3:9–10 Honor the LORD with your wealth, with the firstfruits of all your crops; then your barns will be filled to overflowing, and your vats will brim over with new wine.

   2 Corinthians 9:7 Each man should give what he has decided in his heart to give, not reluctantly or under compulsion, for God loves a cheerful giver.

2. **Those who are wealthy should share with others.**

   1 Timothy 6:17 Command those who are rich in this present world not to be arrogant nor to put their hope in wealth, which is so uncertain, but to put their hope in God, who richly provides us with everything for our enjoyment.

3. **Debts to government and others must be paid.**

   Romans 13:6–8 This is also why you pay taxes, for the authorities are God's servants, who give their full time to governing. Give everyone what you owe him: If you owe taxes, pay taxes; if revenue, then revenue; if respect, then respect; if honor, then honor. Let no debt remain outstanding, except the continuing debt to love one another, for he who loves his fellowman has fulfilled the law.

   Proverbs 22:7 The rich rule over the poor, and the borrower is servant to the lender.

4. **Choices need to be made as to what has priority—God or money.**

   Matthew 6:24 No one can serve two masters. Either he will hate the one and love the other, or he will be devoted to the one and despise the other. You cannot serve both God and Money.

   Hebrews 13:5 Keep your lives free from the love of money and be content with what you have, because God has said, "Never will I leave you; never will I forsake you."

5. **Ultimately, all belongs to God. It is only by his provision we have anything.**

   1 Chronicles 29:11–12 Yours, O LORD, is the greatness and the power and the glory and the majesty and the splendor, for everything in heaven and earth is yours. Yours, O LORD, is the kingdom; you are exalted as head over all. Wealth and honor come from you; you are the ruler of all things. In your hands are strength and power to exalt and give strength to all.

   Deuteronomy 8:18 But remember the LORD your God, for it is he who gives you the ability to produce wealth, and so confirms his covenant, which he swore to your forefathers, as it is today.

   Proverbs 10:22 The blessing of the LORD brings wealth, and he adds no trouble to it.

   1 Timothy 6:17 Command those who are rich in this present world not to be arrogant nor to put their hope in wealth, which is so uncertain, but to put their hope in God, who richly provides us with everything for our enjoyment.

6. **Guard your heart in financial areas.**

   Proverbs 15:16 Better a little with the fear of the LORD than great wealth with turmoil.

   1 Timothy 6:9–10 People who want to get rich fall into temptation and a trap and into many foolish and harmful desires that plunge men into ruin and destruction. For the love of money is a root of all kinds of evil. Some people, eager for money, have wandered from the faith and pierced themselves with many griefs.

Matthew 6:19–21 Do not store up for yourselves treasures on earth, where moth and rust destroy, and where thieves break in and steal. But store up for yourselves treasures in heaven, where moth and rust do not destroy, and where thieves do not break in and steal. For where your treasure is, there your heart will be also.

Flirtation

See also Communication

1. **Beware of those with seductive words.**

   Proverbs 7:4–5 Say to wisdom, "You are my sister," and call understanding your kinsman; they will keep you from the adulteress, from the wayward wife with her seductive words.

   Ephesians 5:4 Nor should there be obscenity, foolish talk or coarse joking, which are out of place, but rather thanksgiving.

   Proverbs 21:23 He who guards his mouth and his tongue keeps himself from calamity.

   Proverbs 6:23–25 For these commands are a lamp, this teaching is a light, and the corrections of discipline are the way to life, keeping you from the immoral woman, from the smooth tongue of the wayward wife. Do not lust in your heart after her beauty or let her captivate you with her eyes.

2. **Beware of being a beautiful woman without discretion.**

   Proverbs 11:22 Like a gold ring in a pig's snout is a beautiful woman who shows no discretion.

3. **Biblical example of seductive woman.**

   Proverbs 7:10–27

4. **Seductive women, in the prophets' time, faced God's discipline.**

   Isaiah 3:16–17 The LORD says, "The women of Zion are haughty, walking along with outstretched necks, flirting with their eyes, tripping along with mincing steps, with ornaments jingling on their ankles. Therefore the Lord will bring sores on the heads of the women of Zion; the LORD will make their scalps bald."

5. **Positive biblical example.**

   1 Peter 3:3–6 Your beauty should not come from outward adornment, such as braided hair and the wearing of gold jewelry and fine clothes. Instead, it should be that of your inner self, the unfading beauty of a gentle and quiet spirit, which is of great worth in God's sight. For this is the way the holy women of the past who put their hope in God used to make themselves beautiful. They were submissive to their own husbands, like Sarah, who obeyed Abraham and called him her master. You are her daughters if you do what is right and do not give way to fear.

Forgiveness

1. God offers forgiveness for any sin.

Isaiah 43:25 I, even I, am he who blots out your transgressions, for my own sake, and remembers your sins no more.

Psalm 103:12 As far as the east is from the west, so far has he removed our transgressions from us.

Lamentations 3:22 Because of the LORD's great love we are not consumed, for his compassions never fail.

Daniel 9:9 The Lord our God is merciful and forgiving, even though we have rebelled against him.

Romans 8:1–2 Therefore, there is now no condemnation for those who are in Christ Jesus, because through Christ Jesus the law of the Spirit of life set me free from the law of sin and death.

Psalm 130:3–4 If you, O LORD, kept a record of sins, O Lord, who could stand? But with you there is forgiveness; therefore you are feared.

Colossians 1:13 For he has rescued us from the dominion of darkness and brought us into the kingdom of the Son he loves.

Isaiah 44:22 I have swept away your offenses like a cloud, your sins like the morning mist. Return to me, for I have redeemed you.

Isaiah 38:17 Surely it was for my benefit that I suffered such anguish. In your love you kept me from the pit of destruction; you have put all my sins behind your back.

Micah 7:18–19 Who is a God like you, who pardons sin and forgives the transgression of the remnant of his inheritance? You do not stay angry forever but delight to show mercy. You will again have compassion on us; you will tread our sins underfoot and hurl all our iniquities into the depths of the sea.

2. Seeking forgiveness.

Psalm 38:18 I confess my iniquity; I am troubled by my sin.

Psalm 51:7 Cleanse me with hyssop, and I will be clean; wash me, and I will be whiter than snow.

Isaiah 55:6–7 Seek the LORD while he may be found; call on him while he is near. Let the wicked forsake his way and the evil man his thoughts. Let him turn to the LORD, and he will have mercy on him, and to our God, for he will freely pardon.

Psalm 32:5 Then I acknowledged my sin to you and did not cover up my iniquity. I said, "I will confess my transgressions to the LORD"—and you forgave the guilt of my sin.

3. Repentance and confession.

1 John 1:9 If we confess our sins, he is faithful and just and will forgive us our sins and purify us from all unrighteousness.

Psalm 66:18 If I had cherished sin in my heart, the Lord would not have listened.

Ephesians 4:22–24 You were taught, with regard to your former way of life, to put off your old self, which is being corrupted by its deceitful desires; to be made new in the attitude of your minds; and to put on the new self, created to be like God in true righteousness and holiness.

4. **Forgiveness and restoration.**

   2 Corinthians 5:17 Therefore, if anyone is in Christ, he is a new creation; the old has gone, the new has come!

5. **Forgiving others.**

   Colossians 3:13 Bear with each other and forgive whatever grievances you may have against one another. Forgive as the Lord forgave you.

   Matthew 6:9–15 This, then, is how you should pray: "Our Father in heaven, hallowed be your name, your kingdom come, your will be done on earth as it is in heaven. Give us today our daily bread. Forgive us our debts, as we also have forgiven our debtors. And lead us not into temptation, but deliver us from the evil one." For if you forgive men when they sin against you, your heavenly Father will also forgive you. But if you do not forgive men their sins, your Father will not forgive your sins.

   Ephesians 4:32 Be kind and compassionate to one another, forgiving each other, just as in Christ God forgave you.

   Matthew 5:23–24 Therefore, if you are offering your gift at the altar and there remember that your brother has something against you, leave your gift there in front of the altar. First go and be reconciled to your brother; then come and offer your gift.

   Luke 23:34 Jesus said, "Father, forgive them, for they do not know what they are doing."

NOTE: No place in Scripture does it mention we are to "forgive" ourselves.

Friendship

1. **Positive aspects of having godly friends.**

   Psalm 133:1 How good and pleasant it is when brothers live together in unity!

   1 Thessalonians 5:11 Therefore encourage one another and build each other up, just as in fact you are doing.

   Hebrews 10:24 And let us consider how we may spur one another on toward love and good deeds.

   Romans 15:7 Accept one another, then, just as Christ accepted you, in order to bring praise to God.

   Ephesians 4:3 Make every effort to keep the unity of the Spirit through the bond of peace.

   Acts 24:16 So I strive always to keep my conscience clear before God and man.

   Acts 2:46–47 Every day they continued to meet together in the temple courts. They broke bread in their homes and ate together with glad and sincere hearts, praising God and enjoying the favor of all the people. And the Lord added to their number daily those who were being saved.

   Philippians 2:4–8 Each of you should look not only to your own interests, but also to the interests of others. Your attitude should be the same as that of Christ Jesus: Who, being in very nature God, did not consider equality with God something to be grasped, but made himself nothing, taking the very nature of a servant, being made in human likeness. And being found in appearance as a man, he humbled himself and became obedient to death—even death on a cross!

Proverbs 17:17 A friend loves at all times, and a brother is born for adversity.

Romans 12:10 Be devoted to one another in brotherly love. Honor one another above yourselves.

Ecclesiastes 4:10 If one falls down, his friend can help him up. But pity the man who falls and has no one to help him up!

Ecclesiastes 4:12 Though one may be overpowered, two can defend themselves. A cord of three strands is not quickly broken.

Galatians 6:2 Carry each other's burdens, and in this way you will fulfill the law of Christ.

2. **Best friends, those of most influence, need to be godly.**

Proverbs 22:24 Do not make friends with a hot-tempered man, do not associate with one easily angered.

Proverbs 23:20 Do not join those who drink too much wine or gorge themselves on meat.

Proverbs 13:20 He who walks with the wise grows wise, but a companion of fools suffers harm.

Proverbs 12:26 A righteous man is cautious in friendship, but the way of the wicked leads them astray.

Exodus 23:2 Do not follow the crowd in doing wrong. When you give testimony in a lawsuit, do not pervert justice by siding with the crowd.

3. **Restoring friendships.**

Romans 12:18 If it is possible, as far as it depends on you, live at peace with everyone.

Proverbs 19:11 A man's wisdom gives him patience; it is to his glory to overlook an offense.

Ephesians 4:32 Be kind and compassionate to one another, forgiving each other, just as in Christ God forgave you.

Matthew 5:23–24 Therefore, if you are offering your gift at the altar and there remember that your brother has something against you, leave your gift there in front of the altar. First go and be reconciled to your brother; then come and offer your gift.

2 Corinthians 5:18 All this is from God, who reconciled us to himself through Christ and gave us the ministry of reconciliation.

2 Timothy 4:2 Preach the Word; be prepared in season and out of season; correct, rebuke and encourage—with great patience and careful instruction.

Philippians 2:1–2 If you have any encouragement from being united with Christ, if any comfort from his love, if any fellowship with the Spirit, if any tenderness and compassion, then make my joy complete by being like-minded, having the same love, being one in spirit and purpose.

God's Will

See also Quiet Time

Determining God's Will in a Situation

1. **Never make a decision contrary to the Word of God.**

   Deuteronomy 5:29 Oh, that their hearts would be inclined to fear me and keep all my commands always, so that it might go well with them and their children forever!

   Proverbs 4:25–27 Let your eyes look straight ahead, fix your gaze directly before you. Make level paths for your feet and take only ways that are firm. Do not swerve to the right or the left; keep your foot from evil.

   Isaiah 55:8 "For my thoughts are not your thoughts, neither are your ways my ways," declares the LORD.

   James 3:17 But the wisdom that comes from heaven is first of all pure; then peace-loving, considerate, submissive, full of mercy and good fruit, impartial and sincere.

2. **Determining God's will involves prayer for self and prayer of others for you.**

   Colossians 1:9–11 For this reason, since the day we heard about you, we have not stopped praying for you and asking God to fill you with the knowledge of his will through all spiritual wisdom and understanding. And we pray this in order that you may live a life worthy of the Lord and may please him in every way: bearing fruit in every good work, growing in the knowledge of God, being strengthened with all power according to his glorious might so that you may have great endurance and patience, and joyfully . . .

James 1:5 If any of you lacks wisdom, he should ask God, who gives generously to all without finding fault, and it will be given to him.

3. **Determining God's will involves the advice of those who are wise.**

   Proverbs 11:14 For lack of guidance a nation falls, but many advisers make victory sure.

   Proverbs 15:22 Plans fail for lack of counsel, but with many advisers they succeed.

4. **Determining God's will involves avoiding sin.**

   1 Thessalonians 4:1–5 Finally, brothers, we instructed you how to live in order to please God, as in fact you are living. Now we ask you and urge you in the Lord Jesus to do this more and more. For you know what instructions we gave you by the authority of the Lord Jesus. It is God's will that you should be sanctified: that you should avoid sexual immorality; that each of you should learn to control his own body in a way that is holy and honorable, not in passionate lust like the heathen, who do not know God.

   Ephesians 5:15–17 Be very careful, then, how you live—not as unwise but as wise, making the most of every opportunity, because the days are evil. Therefore do not be foolish, but understand what the Lord's will is.

5. **Determining God's will involves thankfulness as God leads.**

   Psalm 20:4–5 May he give you the desire of your heart and make all your plans succeed. We will shout for joy when you are victorious and will lift up our banners in the name of our God. May the LORD grant all your requests.

6. **Determining God's will involves proceeding with a yielded heart.**

   Proverbs 3:5–6 Trust in the LORD with all your heart and lean not on your own understanding; in all your ways acknowledge him, and he will make your paths straight.

   Jeremiah 6:16 This is what the LORD says: Stand at the crossroads and look; ask for the ancient paths, ask where the good way is, and walk in it, and you will find rest for your souls.

   Romans 12:1–2 Therefore, I urge you, brothers, in view of God's mercy, to offer your bodies as living sacrifices, holy and pleasing to God—this is your spiritual act of worship. Do not conform any longer to the pattern of this world, but be transformed by the renewing of your mind. Then you will be able to test and approve what God's will is—his good, pleasing and perfect will.

   James 4:13–15 Now listen, you who say, "Today or tomorrow we will go to this or that city, spend a year there, carry on business and make money." Why, you do not even know what will happen tomorrow. What is your life? You are a mist that appears for a little while and then vanishes. Instead, you ought to say, "If it is the Lord's will, we will live and do this or that."

7. **Remember, God is sovereign and has a plan we can have confidence in.**

   Isaiah 25:1 O LORD, you are my God; I will exalt you and praise your name, for in perfect faithfulness you have done marvelous things, things planned long ago.

   Isaiah 42:16 I will lead the blind by ways they have not known, along unfamiliar paths I will guide them; I will turn the darkness into light before them and make the rough places smooth. These are the things I will do; I will not forsake them.

   Jeremiah 29:11 "For I know the plans I have for you," declares the LORD, "plans to prosper you and not to harm you, plans to give you hope and a future."

Psalm 138:8 The LORD will fulfill *his purpose* for me; your love, O LORD, endures forever—do not abandon the works of your hands.

Jeremiah 10:23–24 I know, O LORD, that a man's life is not his own; it is not for man to direct his steps. Correct me, LORD, but only with justice—not in your anger, lest you reduce me to nothing.

8. **The past is full of examples of God's plan being carried through.**

Isaiah 14:24, 27 The LORD Almighty has sworn, "Surely, as I have planned, so it will be, and as I have purposed, so it will stand.". . . For the LORD Almighty has purposed, and who can thwart him? His hand is stretched out, and who can turn it back?

Isaiah 43:13 Yes, and from ancient days I am he. No one can deliver out of my hand. When I act, who can reverse it?

Gossip

See also Communication

1. **Gossip can cause deep hurt to others and ourselves.**

    Proverbs 26:20–22 Without wood a fire goes out; without gossip a quarrel dies down. As charcoal to embers and as wood to fire, so is a quarrelsome man for kindling strife. The words of a gossip are like choice morsels; they go down to a man's inmost parts.

    Proverbs 13:3 He who guards his lips guards his life, but he who speaks rashly will come to ruin.

    Proverbs 20:19 A gossip betrays a confidence; so avoid a man who talks too much.

    Obadiah 1:12 You should not look down on your brother in the day of his misfortune, nor rejoice over the people of Judah in the day of their destruction, nor boast so much in the day of their trouble.

2. **Gossip is a choice we can avoid.**

    Proverbs 17:28 Even a fool is thought wise if he keeps silent, and discerning if he holds his tongue.

1 Peter 3:10 For, "Whoever would love life and see good days must keep his tongue from evil and his lips from deceitful speech."

James 1:26 If anyone considers himself religious and yet does not keep a tight rein on his tongue, he deceives himself and his religion is worthless.

Proverbs 18:21 The tongue has the power of life and death, and those who love it will eat its fruit.

Psalm 141:3 Set a guard over my mouth, O LORD; keep watch over the door of my lips.

James 3:11 Can both fresh water and salt water flow from the same spring?

3. **Gossip and unwholesome speech produce negative qualities.**

Proverbs 10:18 He who conceals his hatred has lying lips, and whoever spreads slander is a fool.

Galatians 5:15 If you keep on biting and devouring each other, watch out or you will be destroyed by each other.

2 Timothy 2:16 Avoid godless chatter, because those who indulge in it will become more and more ungodly.

Proverbs 21:23 He who guards his mouth and his tongue keeps himself from calamity.

4. **Believers must replace gossip with love and the building up of one another.**

Proverbs 17:9 He who covers over an offense promotes love, but whoever repeats the matter separates close friends.

Ephesians 4:29 Do not let any unwholesome talk come out of your mouths, but only what is helpful for building others up according to their needs, that it may benefit those who listen.

Proverbs 16:24 Pleasant words are a honeycomb, sweet to the soul and healing to the bones.

Colossians 4:6 Let your conversation be always full of grace, seasoned with salt, so that you may know how to answer everyone.

5. Principle: Be very careful what you say

   —because it is the right thing to do.

   —because you never know how it will come back to affect you.

   Ecclesiastes 10:20 Do not revile the king even in your thoughts, or curse the rich in your bedroom, because a bird of the air may carry your words, and a bird on the wing may report what you say.

Guilt

See also Forgiveness

1. **Guilt is caused when we do not agree with God about the sin we have done.**

    Psalm 69:5 You know my folly, O God; my guilt is not hidden from you.

2. **We need to admit our sin and seek forgiveness, turning and going in the opposite direction of that sin.**

    1 John 1:8–10 If we claim to be without sin, we deceive ourselves and the truth is not in us. If we confess our sins, he is faithful and just and will forgive us our sins and purify us from all unrighteousness. If we claim we have not sinned, we make him out to be a liar and his word has no place in our lives.

    Hebrews 10:22–23 Let us draw near to God with a sincere heart in full assurance of faith, having our hearts sprinkled to cleanse us from a guilty conscience and having our bodies washed with pure water. Let us hold unswervingly to the hope we profess, for he who promised is faithful.

3. **Replace guilt with proper thinking.**

    Philippians 4:8 Finally, brothers, whatever is true, whatever is noble, whatever is right, whatever is pure, whatever is lovely, whatever is admirable—if anything is excellent or praiseworthy—think about such things.

4. **Guilt is no longer necessary.**

Isaiah 1:18 "Come now, let us reason together," says the LORD. "Though your sins are like scarlet, they shall be as white as snow; though they are red as crimson, they shall be like wool."

Micah 7:18–19 Who is a God like you, who pardons sin and forgives the transgression of the remnant of his inheritance? You do not stay angry forever but delight to show mercy. You will again have compassion on us; you will tread our sins underfoot and hurl all our iniquities into the depths of the sea.

Psalm 103:12 As far as the east is from the west, so far has he removed our transgressions from us.

Isaiah 43:25 I, even I, am he who blots out your transgressions, for my own sake, and remembers your sins no more.

Isaiah 38:17 Surely it was for my benefit that I suffered such anguish. In your love you kept me from the pit of destruction; you have put all my sins behind your back.

Health/Illness

Coping with Present Health Issues

1. The probability of health problems is a part of this present earthly life.

   2 Corinthians 5:4 For while we are in this tent, we groan and are burdened, because we do not wish to be unclothed but to be clothed with our heavenly dwelling, so that what is mortal may be swallowed up by life. [Metaphor concerning the frailty of this earthly body and the longing for immortality]

2. Ingredients that improve health are:

   Proverbs 14:30 A heart at peace gives life to the body, but envy rots the bones.

   Proverbs 18:14 A man's spirit sustains him in sickness, but a crushed spirit who can bear?

   Proverbs 17:22 A cheerful heart is good medicine, but a crushed spirit dries up the bones.

3. We do not walk through health problems alone.

   Philippians 4:19 And my God will meet all your needs according to his glorious riches in Christ Jesus.

2 Corinthians 4:16 Therefore we do not lose heart. Though outwardly we are wasting away, yet inwardly we are being renewed day by day.

4. **Whether or not a present illness may or may not lead to death, we need to bring glory to God through it.**

    Psalm 119:71 It was good for me to be afflicted so that I might learn your decrees.

    2 Corinthians 12:9–10 But he said to me, "My grace is sufficient for you, for my power is made perfect in weakness." Therefore I will boast all the more gladly about my weaknesses, so that Christ's power may rest on me. That is why, for Christ's sake, I delight in weaknesses, in insults, in hardships, in persecutions, in difficulties. For when I am weak, then I am strong.

    1 Peter 1:6–7 In this you greatly rejoice, though now for a little while you may have had to suffer grief in all kinds of trials. These have come so that your faith—of greater worth than gold, which perishes even though refined by fire—may be proved genuine and may result in praise, glory and honor when Jesus Christ is revealed.

5. **God provides strength.**

    2 Samuel 22:33 It is God who arms me with strength and makes my way perfect.

    Psalm 73:26 My flesh and my heart may fail, but God is the strength of my heart and my portion forever.

    2 Corinthians 4:7–9 But we have this treasure in jars of clay to show that this all-surpassing power is from God and not from us. We are hard pressed on every side, but not crushed; perplexed, but not in despair; persecuted, but not abandoned; struck down, but not destroyed.

    Psalm 91:4 He will cover you with his feathers, and under his wings you will find refuge; his faithfulness will be your shield and rampart.

    Isaiah 40:30–31 Even youths grow tired and weary, and young men stumble and fall; but those who hope in the LORD will renew their strength. They will soar on wings like eagles; they will run and not grow weary, they will walk and not be faint.

6. **Illness, as a trial, develops character.**

   James 1:2–4 Consider it pure joy, my brothers, whenever you face trials of many kinds, because you know that the testing of your faith develops perseverance. Perseverance must finish its work so that you may be mature and complete, not lacking anything.

   Job 23:8–10 But if I go to the east, he is not there; if I go to the west, I do not find him. When he is at work in the north, I do not see him; when he turns to the south, I catch no glimpse of him. But he knows the way that I take; when he has tested me, I will come forth as gold.

Fear of Health Problems

1. **Do not place confidence in self—avoid evil.**

   Proverbs 3:7–8 Do not be wise in your own eyes; fear the LORD and shun evil. This will bring health to your body and nourishment to your bones.

2. **Final future hope of freedom from pain and illness.**

   Revelation 21:4 He will wipe every tear from their eyes. There will be no more death or mourning or crying or pain, for the old order of things has passed away.

   Philippians 3:20–21 But our citizenship is in heaven. And we eagerly await a Savior from there, the Lord Jesus Christ, who, by the power that enables him to bring everything under his control, will transform our lowly bodies so that they will be like his glorious body.

NOTE: It would be beneficial to have the counselee see a physician.

Homosexual/Lesbian

See also Sexual Purity

1. **Homosexual activity is sinful and sexually impure.**

Romans 1:24–27 Therefore God gave them over in the sinful desires of their hearts to sexual impurity for the degrading of their bodies with one another. They exchanged the truth of God for a lie, and worshiped and served created things rather than the Creator—who is forever praised. Amen. Because of this, God gave them over to shameful lusts. Even their women exchanged natural relations for unnatural ones. In the same way the men also abandoned natural relations with women and were inflamed with lust for one another. Men committed indecent acts with other men, and received in themselves the due penalty for their perversion.

Jude 1:7 In a similar way, Sodom and Gomorrah and the surrounding towns gave themselves up to sexual immorality and perversion. They serve as an example of those who suffer the punishment of eternal fire.

Leviticus 20:13 If a man lies with a man as one lies with a woman, both of them have done what is detestable.

Leviticus 18:22 Do not lie with a man as one lies with a woman; that is detestable.

Romans 8:5–8 Those who live according to the sinful nature have their minds set on what that nature desires; but those who live in accordance with the Spirit have their minds set on what the Spirit desires. The mind of sinful man is death, but the mind controlled by the Spirit is life and peace; the sinful mind is hostile to God. It does not submit to God's law, nor can it do so. Those controlled by the sinful nature cannot please God.

Galatians 5:19–21 The acts of the sinful nature are obvious: sexual immorality, impurity and debauchery; idolatry and witchcraft; hatred, discord, jealousy, fits of rage, selfish ambition, dissensions, factions and envy; drunkenness, orgies, and the like. I warn you, as I did before, that those who live like this will not inherit the kingdom of God.

2. **While homosexual activity is sin and impure, it is possible with God's help to change.**

    1 Corinthians 6:9–11 Do you not know that the wicked will not inherit the kingdom of God? Do not be deceived: Neither the sexually immoral nor idolaters nor adulterers nor male prostitutes nor homosexual offenders nor thieves nor the greedy nor drunkards nor slanderers nor swindlers will inherit the kingdom of God. And that is what some of you were. But you were washed, you were sanctified, you were justified in the name of the Lord Jesus Christ and by the Spirit of our God.

    Romans 7:23–25 But I see another law at work in the members of my body, waging war against the law of my mind and making me a prisoner of the law of sin at work within my members. What a wretched man I am! Who will rescue me from this body of death? Thanks be to God—through Jesus Christ our Lord! So then, I myself in my mind am a slave to God's law, but in the sinful nature a slave to the law of sin.

    Romans 6:19 I put this in human terms because you are weak in your natural selves. Just as you used to offer the parts of your body in slavery to impurity and to ever-increasing wickedness, so now offer them in slavery to righteousness leading to holiness.

    Galatians 5:16 So I say, live by the Spirit, and you will not gratify the desires of the sinful nature.

1 Peter 4:1–3 Therefore, since Christ suffered in his body, arm yourselves also with the same attitude, because he who has suffered in his body is done with sin. As a result, he does not live the rest of his earthly life for evil human desires, but rather for the will of God. For you have spent enough time in the past doing what pagans choose to do—living in debauchery, lust, drunkenness, orgies, carousing and detestable idolatry.

3. **Moral choices must be made.**

James 4:17 Anyone, then, who knows the good he ought to do and doesn't do it, sins.

Psalm 141:4 Let not my heart be drawn to what is evil, to take part in wicked deeds with men who are evildoers; let me not eat of their delicacies.

Romans 12:1–2 Therefore, I urge you, brothers, in view of God's mercy, to offer your bodies as living sacrifices, holy and pleasing to God—this is your spiritual act of worship. Do not conform any longer to the pattern of this world, but be transformed by the renewing of your mind. Then you will be able to test and approve what God's will is—his good, pleasing and perfect will.

1 Thessalonians 4:1–8 Finally, brothers, we instructed you how to live in order to please God, as in fact you are living. Now we ask you and urge you in the Lord Jesus to do this more and more. For you know what instructions we gave you by the authority of the Lord Jesus. It is God's will that you should be sanctified: that you should avoid sexual immorality; that each of you should learn to control his own body in a way that is holy and honorable, not in passionate lust like the heathen, who do not know God; and that in this matter no one should wrong his brother or take advantage of him. The Lord will punish men for all such sins, as we have already told you and warned you. For God did not call us to be impure, but to live a holy life. Therefore, he who rejects this instruction does not reject man but God, who gives you his Holy Spirit.

Hospitality

1. **Biblical examples.**

   2 Timothy 1:16 May the Lord show mercy to the household of Onesiphorus, because he often refreshed me and was not ashamed of my chains.

   3 John 1:5–6 Dear friend, you are faithful in what you are doing for the brothers, even though they are strangers to you. They have told the church about your love. You will do well to send them on their way in a manner worthy of God.

2. **Biblical command.**

   Romans 12:13 Share with God's people who are in need. Practice hospitality.

   1 Peter 4:9 Offer hospitality to one another without grumbling.

   Hebrews 13:2 Do not forget to entertain strangers, for by so doing some people have entertained angels without knowing it.

3. **Principles for hospitality.**

   Proverbs 11:25 A generous man will prosper; he who refreshes others will himself be refreshed.

   Acts 2:46–47 Every day they continued to meet together in the temple courts. They broke bread in their homes and ate together with glad and sincere hearts, praising God and enjoying the favor of all the people. And the Lord added to their number daily those who were being saved.

Proverbs 3:27 Do not withhold good from those who deserve it, when it is in your power to act.

Proverbs 22:9 A generous man will himself be blessed, for he shares his food with the poor.

1 Peter 4:11 If anyone speaks, he should do it as one speaking the very words of God. If anyone serves, he should do it with the strength God provides, so that in all things God may be praised through Jesus Christ. To him be the glory and the power for ever and ever. Amen.

4. Hospitality is a quality of leaders.

1 Timothy 3:2 Now the overseer must be above reproach, the husband of but one wife, temperate, self-controlled, respectable, hospitable, able to teach.

Infertility

1. Hannah's example of prayer for a child.

1 Samuel 1:27–28 I prayed for this child, and the LORD has granted me what I asked of him. So now I give him to the LORD. For his whole life he will be given over to the LORD.

2. God understands everything, including the depth of barrenness.

Isaiah 54:1 "Sing, O barren woman, you who never bore a child; burst into song, shout for joy, you who were never in labor; because more are the children of the desolate woman than of her who has a husband," says the LORD.

Psalm 94:19 When anxiety was great within me, your consolation brought joy to my soul.

Psalm 69:1–3 Save me, O God, for the waters have come up to my neck. I sink in the miry depths, where there is no foothold. I have come into the deep waters; the floods engulf me. I am worn out calling for help; my throat is parched. My eyes fail, looking for my God.

Psalm 142:3 When my spirit grows faint within me, it is you who know my way.

Proverbs 30:15–16 There are three things that are never satisfied, four that never say, 'Enough!': the grave, the barren womb, land, which is never satisfied with water, and fire, which never says, 'Enough!'

3. **Confidence needs to be placed fully in God, trusting him for the possibility of a future without children.**

   Habakkuk 3:17–19 Though the fig tree does not bud and there are no grapes on the vines, though the olive crop fails and the fields produce no food, though there are no sheep in the pen and no cattle in the stalls, yet I will rejoice in the LORD, I will be joyful in God my Savior. The Sovereign LORD is my strength; he makes my feet like the feet of a deer, he enables me to go on the heights.

   2 Corinthians 12:9 But he said to me, "My grace is sufficient for you, for my power is made perfect in weakness." Therefore I will boast all the more gladly about my weaknesses, so that Christ's power may rest on me.

   Isaiah 40:29 He gives strength to the weary and increases the power of the weak.

   Isaiah 55:8–9 "For my thoughts are not your thoughts, neither are your ways my ways," declares the LORD. "As the heavens are higher than the earth, so are my ways higher than your ways and my thoughts than your thoughts."

NOTE: It would be beneficial to have the counselee see a specialist in this area.

Laziness

See also Organization/Time Management

1. **Laziness promotes problems.**

   Proverbs 10:4 Lazy hands make a man poor, but diligent hands bring wealth.

   Proverbs 12:24 Diligent hands will rule, but laziness ends in slave labor.

   Proverbs 13:4 The sluggard craves and gets nothing, but the desires of the diligent are fully satisfied.

   Proverbs 20:4 A sluggard does not plow in season; so at harvest time he looks but finds nothing.

   Ecclesiastes 10:18 If a man is lazy, the rafters sag; if his hands are idle, the house leaks.

   Proverbs 19:15 Laziness brings on deep sleep, and the shiftless man goes hungry.

2. **We are commanded to work and not be lazy.**

   Ecclesiastes 9:10 Whatever your hand finds to do, do it with all your might, for in the grave, where you are going, there is neither working nor planning nor knowledge nor wisdom.

   2 Thessalonians 3:10–12 For even when we were with you, we gave you this rule: "If a man will not work, he shall not eat." We hear that some among you are idle. They are not busy; they are busybodies. Such people we command and urge in the Lord Jesus Christ to settle down and earn the bread they eat.

Hebrews 6:12 We do not want you to become lazy, but to imitate those who through faith and patience inherit what has been promised.

3. **Proper responsibility in work is serving the Lord.**

   Romans 12:11 Never be lacking in zeal, but keep your spiritual fervor, serving the Lord.

   1 Corinthians 15:58 Therefore, my dear brothers, stand firm. Let nothing move you. Always give yourselves fully to the work of the Lord, because you know that your labor in the Lord is not in vain.

   Galatians 6:9 Let us not become weary in doing good, for at the proper time we will reap a harvest if we do not give up.

4. **Proper care of home and family is serving the Lord.**

   Proverbs 31:27 She watches over the affairs of her household and does not eat the bread of idleness.

   Titus 2:3–5 Likewise, teach the older women to be reverent in the way they live, not to be slanderers or addicted to much wine, but to teach what is good. Then they can train the younger women to love their husbands and children, to be self-controlled and pure, to be busy at home, to be kind, and to be subject to their husbands, so that no one will malign the word of God.

   1 Corinthians 4:2 Now it is required that those who have been given a trust must prove faithful.

   Proverbs 14:1 The wise woman builds her house, but with her own hands the foolish one tears hers down.

For further reference see 1 Timothy 5:8–14 and Proverbs 31:7–31.

5. **Summary passage on laziness**

   2 Thessalonians 3:6–9 In the name of the Lord Jesus Christ, we command you, brothers, to keep away from every brother who is idle and does not live according to the teaching you received from us. For you yourselves know how you ought to follow our example. We were not idle when we were with you, nor did we eat anyone's food without paying for it. On the contrary, we worked night and day, laboring and toiling so that we would not be a burden to any of you. We did this, not because we do not have the right to such help, but in order to make ourselves a model for you to follow.

Loneliness

1. **The problem of loneliness.**

   Psalm 102:7–11 I lie awake; I have become like a bird alone on a roof. All day long my enemies taunt me; those who rail against me use my name as a curse. For I eat ashes as my food and mingle my drink with tears because of your great wrath, for you have taken me up and thrown me aside. My days are like the evening shadow; I wither away like grass.

2. **David turned to God when he was lonely.**

   Psalm 25:16 Turn to me and be gracious to me, for I am lonely and afflicted.

   Psalm 142:1–4 I cry aloud to the LORD; I lift up my voice to the LORD for mercy. I pour out my complaint before him; before him I tell my trouble. When my spirit grows faint within me, it is you who know my way. In the path where I walk men have hidden a snare for me. Look to my right and see; no one is concerned for me. I have no refuge; no one cares for my life.

3. **God will provide for us when we feel alone.**

   Psalm 68:5–6 A father to the fatherless, a defender of widows, is God in his holy dwelling. God sets the lonely in families, he leads forth the prisoners with singing; but the rebellious live in a sun-scorched land.

Deuteronomy 31:6 Be strong and courageous. Do not be afraid or terrified because of them, for the LORD your God goes with you; he will never leave you nor forsake you.

John 15:4 Remain in me, and I will remain in you. No branch can bear fruit by itself; it must remain in the vine. Neither can you bear fruit unless you remain in me.

Psalm 38:9–15 All my longings lie open before you, O Lord; my sighing is not hidden from you. My heart pounds, my strength fails me; even the light has gone from my eyes. My friends and companions avoid me because of my wounds; my neighbors stay far away. Those who seek my life set their traps, those who would harm me talk of my ruin; all day long they plot deception. I am like a deaf man, who cannot hear, like a mute, who cannot open his mouth; I have become like a man who does not hear, whose mouth can offer no reply. I wait for you, O LORD; you will answer, O Lord my God.

Hebrews 13:5 Keep your lives free from the love of money and be content with what you have, because God has said, "Never will I leave you; never will I forsake you."

For further reference see Psalm 62:1–6.

Lust

See also Fantasizing

1. **Lust is a sinful desire that begins in the mind.**

   Matthew 5:28 But I tell you that anyone who looks at a woman lustfully has already committed adultery with her in his heart.

   1 Peter 2:11 Dear friends, I urge you, as aliens and strangers in the world, to abstain from sinful desires, which war against your soul.

2. **Lust is caused by lack of obedience to God's Word.**

   Mark 4:19 But the worries of this life, the deceitfulness of wealth and the desires for other things come in and choke the word, making it unfruitful.

   Ephesians 4:22 You were taught, with regard to your former way of life, to put off your old self, which is being corrupted by its deceitful desires.

   2 Timothy 4:3–4 For the time will come when men will not put up with sound doctrine. Instead, to suit their own desires, they will gather around them a great number of teachers to say what their itching ears want to hear. They will turn their ears away from the truth and turn aside to myths.

3. **Each person must guard himself for what is his own individual area of lusting.**

   James 1:14–15 But each one is tempted when, by his own evil desire, he is dragged away and enticed. Then, after desire has conceived, it gives birth to sin; and sin, when it is full-grown, gives birth to death.

   Job 31:1 I made a covenant with my eyes not to look lustfully at a girl.

   1 Thessalonians 4:3–5 It is God's will that you should be sanctified: that you should avoid sexual immorality; that each of you should learn to control his own body in a way that is holy and honorable, not in passionate lust like the heathen, who do not know God.

4. **It is possible to avoid lustful thoughts.**

   2 Timothy 2:22 Flee the evil desires of youth, and pursue righteousness, faith, love and peace, along with those who call on the Lord out of a pure heart.

   Titus 2:12 It teaches us to say "No" to ungodliness and worldly passions, and to live self-controlled, upright and godly lives in this present age.

   1 Corinthians 10:13 No temptation has seized you except what is common to man. And God is faithful; he will not let you be tempted beyond what you can bear. But when you are tempted, he will also provide a way out so that you can stand up under it.

Lying

See also Communication

1. **Recognize that lying is always wrong.**

   Exodus 20:16 You shall not give false testimony against your neighbor.

   Colossians 3:9 Do not lie to each other, since you have taken off your old self with its practices.

2. **Lying is a sin that is a struggle from one's youth.**

   Psalm 58:3 Even from birth the wicked go astray; from the womb they are wayward and speak lies.

   Romans 1:25 They exchanged the truth of God for a lie, and worshiped and served created things rather than the Creator.

3. **God hates lying.**

   Psalm 5:6 You destroy those who tell lies; bloodthirsty and deceitful men the LORD abhors.

   Psalm 31:18 Let their lying lips be silenced, for with pride and contempt they speak arrogantly against the righteous.

   Proverbs 12:22 The LORD detests lying lips, but he delights in men who are truthful.

4. **Lying is not a choice for the believer.**

   Psalm 34:13 Keep your tongue from evil and your lips from speaking lies.

5. **Telling the truth is God's way.**

Ephesians 4:25 Therefore each of you must put off falsehood and speak truthfully to his neighbor, for we are all members of one body.

Colossians 3:9 Do not lie to each other, since you have taken off your old self with its practices.

1 John 2:21 I do not write to you because you do not know the truth, but because you do know it and because no lie comes from the truth.

Psalm 15:1–2 LORD, who may dwell in your sanctuary? Who may live on your holy hill? He whose walk is blameless and who does what is righteous, who speaks the truth from his heart.

Marriage

See also Sex Life, Submission

1. **Marriage originated as a part of God's design for humankind.**

    Genesis 2:18, 22–25 The LORD God said, "It is not good for the man to be alone. I will make a helper suitable for him.". . . Then the LORD God made a woman from the rib he had taken out of the man, and he brought her to the man. The man said, "This is now bone of my bones and flesh of my flesh; she shall be called 'woman', for she was taken out of man." For this reason a man will leave his father and mother and be united to his wife, and they will become one flesh. The man and his wife were both naked, and they felt no shame.

2. **Marriage is an honorable union.**

    Hebrews 13:4 Marriage should be honored by all, and the marriage bed kept pure, for God will judge the adulterer and all the sexually immoral.

3. **Believers should only marry other believers.**

    2 Corinthians 6:14 Do not be yoked together with unbelievers. For what do righteousness and wickedness have in common? Or what fellowship can light have with darkness?

4. **Marriage is a permanent covenant for life.**

Mark 10:7–9 "For this reason a man will leave his father and mother and be united to his wife, and the two will become one flesh." So they are no longer two, but one. Therefore what God has joined together, let man not separate.

Matthew 19:6 So they are no longer two, but one. Therefore what God has joined together, let man not separate.

Malachi 2:14 You ask, "Why?" It is because the LORD is acting as the witness between you and the wife of your youth, because you have broken faith with her, though she is your partner, the wife of your marriage covenant.

5. **Marriage operates best when God's blueprint is followed.**

See 1 Corinthians 7.

Husband—loving leader

Colossians 3:19 Husbands, love your wives and do not be harsh with them.

Proverbs 18:22 He who finds a wife finds what is good and receives favor from the LORD.

1 Corinthians 7:2 But since there is so much immorality, each man should have his own wife, and each woman her own husband.

Ephesians 5:25–33 Husbands, love your wives, just as Christ loved the church and gave himself up for her to make her holy, cleansing her by the washing with water through the word, and to present her to himself as a radiant church, without stain or wrinkle or any other blemish, but holy and blameless. In this same way, husbands ought to love their wives as their own bodies. He who loves his wife loves himself. After all, no one ever hated his own body, but he feeds and cares for it, just as Christ does the church—for we are members of his body. "For this reason a man will leave his father and mother and be united to his wife, and the two will become one flesh." This is a profound mystery—but I am talking about Christ and the church. However, each one of you also must love his wife as he loves himself, and the wife must respect her husband.

Wife—respectful completer

Colossians 3:18 Wives, submit to your husbands, as is fitting in the Lord.

Ephesians 5:22–23 Wives, submit to your husbands as to the Lord. For the husband is the head of the wife as Christ is the head of the church, his body, of which he is the Savior.

Proverbs 14:1 The wise woman builds her house, but with her own hands the foolish one tears hers down.

Proverbs 12:4 A wife of noble character is her husband's crown, but a disgraceful wife is like decay in his bones.

Proverbs 19:13–14 A foolish son is his father's ruin, and a quarrelsome wife is like a constant dripping. Houses and wealth are inherited from parents, but a prudent wife is from the LORD.

Proverbs 25:24 Better to live on a corner of the roof than share a house with a quarrelsome wife.

Proverbs 21:9, 19 Better to live on a corner of the roof than share a house with a quarrelsome wife. . . .Better to live in a desert than with a quarrelsome and ill-tempered wife.

Proverbs 27:15–16 A quarrelsome wife is like a constant dripping on a rainy day; restraining her is like restraining the wind or grasping oil with the hand.

Materialism

See also Contentment

1. **The desire for more possessions leads to a trap of destruction.**

   1 Timothy 6:6–9 But godliness with contentment is great gain. For we brought nothing into the world, and we can take nothing out of it. But if we have food and clothing, we will be content with that. People who want to get rich fall into temptation and a trap and into many foolish and harmful desires that plunge men into ruin and destruction.

   James 5:1–5 Now listen, you rich people, weep and wail because of the misery that is coming upon you. Your wealth has rotted, and moths have eaten your clothes. Your gold and silver are corroded. Their corrosion will testify against you and eat your flesh like fire. You have hoarded wealth in the last days. Look! The wages you failed to pay the workmen who mowed your fields are crying out against you. The cries of the harvesters have reached the ears of the Lord Almighty. You have lived on earth in luxury and self-indulgence. You have fattened yourselves in the day of slaughter.

   Proverbs 28:25–26 A greedy man stirs up dissension, but he who trusts in the LORD will prosper. He who trusts in himself is a fool, but he who walks in wisdom is kept safe.

   Proverbs 23:4 Do not wear yourself out to get rich; have the wisdom to show restraint.

2. **Desire for riches can sidetrack individuals from their beliefs.**

   1 Timothy 6:10 For the love of money is a root of all kinds of evil. Some people, eager for money, have wandered from the faith and pierced themselves with many griefs.

   1 John 2:15 Do not love the world or anything in the world. If anyone loves the world, the love of the Father is not in him.

   Proverbs 30:8–9 Keep falsehood and lies far from me; give me neither poverty nor riches, but give me only my daily bread. Otherwise, I may have too much and disown you and say, "Who is the LORD?" Or I may become poor and steal, and so dishonor the name of my God.

   Matthew 19:24 Again I tell you, it is easier for a camel to go through the eye of a needle than for a rich man to enter the kingdom of God.

3. **Security is not found in possessions.**

   1 Timothy 6:17 Command those who are rich in this present world not to be arrogant nor to put their hope in wealth, which is so uncertain, but to put their hope in God, who richly provides us with everything for our enjoyment.

   Isaiah 58:11 The LORD will guide you always; he will satisfy your needs in a sun-scorched land and will strengthen your frame. You will be like a well-watered garden, like a spring whose waters never fail.

   Luke 12:15 Then he said to them, "Watch out! Be on your guard against all kinds of greed; a man's life does not consist in the abundance of his possessions."

For further reference see Matthew 6:25–34.

4. **Those blessed materially need to help those less fortunate.**

   Proverbs 31:8–9 "Speak up for those who cannot speak for themselves, for the rights of all who are destitute. Speak up and judge fairly; defend the rights of the poor and needy."

1 Timothy 6:18–19 Command them to do good, to be rich in good deeds, and to be generous and willing to share. In this way they will lay up treasure for themselves as a firm foundation for the coming age, so that they may take hold of the life that is truly life.

5. **Solution for avoiding materialism.**

1 Timothy 6:10–11 For the love of money is a root of all kinds of evil. Some people, eager for money, have wandered from the faith and pierced themselves with many griefs. But you, man of God, flee from all this, and pursue righteousness, godliness, faith, love, endurance and gentleness.

Colossians 3:12 Therefore, as God's chosen people, holy and dearly loved, clothe yourselves with compassion, kindness, humility, gentleness and patience.

Matthew 6:19–21 Do not store up for yourselves treasures on earth, where moth and rust destroy, and where thieves break in and steal. But store up for yourselves treasures in heaven, where moth and rust do not destroy, and where thieves do not break in and steal. For where your treasure is, there your heart will be also.

Philippians 4:11–13 I am not saying this because I am in need, for I have learned to be content whatever the circumstances. I know what it is to be in need, and I know what it is to have plenty. I have learned the secret of being content in any and every situation, whether well fed or hungry, whether living in plenty or in want. I can do everything through him who gives me strength.

Menopause/Aging

1. **No direct mention, but principles for aging of which menopause is a part.**

    Isaiah 46:4 Even to your old age and gray hairs I am he, I am he who will sustain you. I have made you and I will carry you; I will sustain you and I will rescue you.

    Isaiah 35:3–4 Strengthen the feeble hands, steady the knees that give way; say to those with fearful hearts, "Be strong, do not fear; your God will come, he will come with vengeance; with divine retribution he will come to save you."

    Proverbs 16:31 Gray hair is a crown of splendor; it is attained by a righteous life.

    Proverbs 20:29 The glory of young men is their strength, gray hair the splendor of the old.

2. **God understands every stage of life and is worthy of our trust.**

    Psalm 31:14–15 But I trust in you, O LORD; I say, "You are my God." My times are in your hands.

3. **God provides for every time of life.**

    Isaiah 58:11 The LORD will guide you always; he will satisfy your needs in a sun-scorched land and will strengthen your frame. You will be like a well-watered garden, like a spring whose waters never fail.

Job 12:12 Is not wisdom found among the aged? Does not long life bring understanding?

Psalm 71:9, 18 Do not cast me away when I am old; do not forsake me when my strength is gone. . . . Even when I am old and gray, do not forsake me, O God, till I declare your power to the next generation, your might to all who are to come.

Philippians 4:13 I can do everything through him who gives me strength.

4. **Old age should be a productive time.**

Titus 2:3–5 Likewise, teach the older women to be reverent in the way they live, not to be slanderers or addicted to much wine, but to teach what is good. Then they can train the younger women to love their husbands and children, to be self-controlled and pure, to be busy at home, to be kind, and to be subject to their husbands, so that no one will malign the word of God.

Psalm 92:12–15 The righteous will flourish like a palm tree, they will grow like a cedar of Lebanon; planted in the house of the LORD, they will flourish in the courts of our God. They will still bear fruit in old age, they will stay fresh and green, proclaiming, "The LORD is upright; he is my Rock, and there is no wickedness in him."

NOTE: It would be beneficial to have the counselee see a physician.

Miscarriage

See also God's Will, Death/Grief

1. **During a difficult time, we need to trust God's sovereignty.**

   Psalm 69:29–30 I am in pain and distress; may your salvation, O God, protect me. I will praise God's name in song and glorify him with thanksgiving.

   Psalm 18:30 As for God, his way is perfect; the word of the LORD is flawless. He is a shield for all who take refuge in him.

2. **The unborn child is safe in God's care.**

   Isaiah 49:1 Listen to me, you islands; hear this, you distant nations: Before I was born the LORD called me; from my birth he has made mention of my name.

   Psalm 139:13–16 For you created my inmost being; you knit me together in my mother's womb. I praise you because I am fearfully and wonderfully made; your works are wonderful, I know that full well. My frame was not hidden from you when I was made in the secret place. When I was woven together in the depths of the earth, your eyes saw my unformed body. All the days ordained for me were written in your book before one of them came to be.

3. **God understands with a tender heart our grief.**

   Psalm 40:1 I waited patiently for the LORD; he turned to me and heard my cry.

2 Corinthians 1:3–4 Praise be to the God and Father of our Lord Jesus Christ, the Father of compassion and the God of all comfort, who comforts us in all our troubles, so that we can comfort those in any trouble with the comfort we ourselves have received from God.

Isaiah 25:8 He will swallow up death forever. The Sovereign LORD will wipe away the tears from all faces; he will remove the disgrace of his people from all the earth. The LORD has spoken.

Psalm 18:1–6 I love you, O LORD, my strength. The LORD is my rock, my fortress and my deliverer; my God is my rock, in whom I take refuge. He is my shield and the horn of my salvation, my stronghold. I call to the LORD, who is worthy of praise, and I am saved from my enemies. The cords of death entangled me; the torrents of destruction overwhelmed me. The cords of the grave coiled around me; the snares of death confronted me. In my distress I called to the LORD; I cried to my God for help. From his temple he heard my voice; my cry came before him, into his ears.

For further reference see Psalm 139:1–18.

Mothering

See also Disciplining Children, Training Children

1. **Tender parenting is a frequent theme of Scripture.**

    Isaiah 40:11 He tends his flock like a shepherd: He gathers the lambs in his arms and carries them close to his heart; he gently leads those that have young.

    Isaiah 49:15 Can a mother forget the baby at her breast and have no compassion on the child she has borne? Though she may forget, I will not forget you!

    Isaiah 66:13 As a mother comforts her child, so will I comfort you; and you will be comforted over Jerusalem.

    1 Thessalonians 2:7 But we were gentle among you, like a mother caring for her little children.

2. **Mothers are to be honored.**

    Exodus 20:12 Honor your father and your mother, so that you may live long in the land the LORD your God is giving you.

    Proverbs 23:22 Listen to your father, who gave you life, and do not despise your mother when she is old.

Matthew 15:4 For God said, 'Honor your father and mother' and 'Anyone who curses his father or mother must be put to death.'

Ephesians 6:2 "Honor your father and mother"—which is the first commandment with a promise.

3. Qualities for mothers:

Love of husbands and children, self-control, keepers of home, kind, submissive

Titus 2:3–5 Likewise, teach the older women to be reverent in the way they live, not to be slanderers or addicted to much wine, but to teach what is good. Then they can train the younger women to love their husbands and children, to be self-controlled and pure, to be busy at home, to be kind, and to be subject to their husbands, so that no one will malign the word of God.

Humble, gentle, patient, loving

Ephesians 4:2 Be completely humble and gentle; be patient, bearing with one another in love.

Fruit of the Spirit

Galatians 5:22–23 But the fruit of the Spirit is love, joy, peace, patience, kindness, goodness, faithfulness, gentleness and self-control. Against such things there is no law.

Building up, kind, compassionate, forgiving

Ephesians 4:29–32 Do not let any unwholesome talk come out of your mouths, but only what is helpful for building others up according to their needs, that it may benefit those who listen. And do not grieve the Holy Spirit of God, with whom you were sealed for the day of redemption. Get rid of all bitterness, rage and anger, brawling and slander, along with every form of malice. Be kind and compassionate to one another, forgiving each other, just as in Christ God forgave you.

Sympathetic, loving, compassionate, humble

1 Peter 3:8–9 Finally, all of you, live in harmony with one another; be sympathetic, love as brothers, be compassionate and humble. Do not repay evil with evil or insult with insult, but with blessing, because to this you were called so that you may inherit a blessing.

Organization/Time Management

See also Laziness

1. **God desires that we are wise in the use of our time.**

    Psalm 90:12 Teach us to number our days aright, that we may gain a heart of wisdom.

    Ephesians 5:15–18 Be very careful, then, how you live—not as unwise but as wise, making the most of every opportunity, because the days are evil. Therefore do not be foolish, but understand what the Lord's will is. Do not get drunk on wine, which leads to debauchery. Instead, be filled with the Spirit.

    Psalm 39:4 Show me, O LORD, my life's end and the number of my days; let me know how fleeting is my life.

2. **God desires that life be managed with order.**

    1 Corinthians 14:40 But everything should be done in a fitting and orderly way.

3. **One of the spiritual gifts is administration.**

    1 Corinthians 12:28 And in the church God has appointed first of all apostles, second prophets, third teachers, then workers of miracles, also those having gifts of healing, those able to help others, those with gifts of administration, and those speaking in different kinds of tongues.

4. **What we do should bring honor to God.**

   Colossians 3:17 And whatever you do, whether in word or deed, do it all in the name of the Lord Jesus, giving thanks to God the Father through him.

   1 Corinthians 15:58 Therefore, my dear brothers, stand firm. Let nothing move you. Always give yourselves fully to the work of the Lord, because you know that your labor in the Lord is not in vain.

5. **Our work should entail doing our best.**

   Ecclesiastes 9:10 Whatever your hand finds to do, do it with all your might.

6. **Completion of a job well done is not only because of our skills, but also because of God's blessing.**

   Psalm 90:17 May the favor of the Lord our God rest upon us; establish the work of our hands for us—yes, establish the work of our hands.

7. **Staying balanced is crucial in managing time.**

   Ecclesiastes 7:18 It is good to grasp the one and not let go of the other. The man who fears God will avoid all extremes.

8. **Delegation of responsibilities is a biblical concept.**

   Exodus 18:18, 21–22 You and these people who come to you will only wear yourselves out. The work is too heavy for you; you cannot handle it alone. . . . But select capable men from all the people—men who fear God, trustworthy men who hate dishonest gain—and appoint them as officials over thousands, hundreds, fifties and tens. Have them serve as judges for the people at all times, but have them bring every difficult case to you; the simple cases they can decide themselves. That will make your load lighter, because they will share it with you.

For further reference see: Deuteronomy 1:9–15.

Orphan

1. As human parents are not able to be a part of a life, our heavenly Father is certainly actively involved.

    Psalm 27:10 Though my father and mother forsake me, the LORD will receive me.

    2 Corinthians 6:18 "I will be a Father to you, and you will be my sons and daughters, says the Lord Almighty."

    Isaiah 49:15–16 Can a mother forget the baby at her breast and have no compassion on the child she has borne? Though she may forget, I will not forget you! See, I have engraved you on the palms of my hands; your walls are ever before me.

    Isaiah 66:13 As a mother comforts her child, so will I comfort you; and you will be comforted over Jerusalem.

    Jeremiah 31:3 The LORD appeared to us in the past, saying: "I have loved you with an everlasting love; I have drawn you with loving-kindness."

    Job 29:12 Because I rescued the poor who cried for help, and the fatherless who had none to assist him.

2. God has a concern for those without parents and many times instructs others to defend and care for them.

    Psalm 82:3–4 Defend the cause of the weak and fatherless; maintain the rights of the poor and oppressed. Rescue the weak and needy; deliver them from the hand of the wicked.

Psalm 146:9 The LORD watches over the alien and sustains the fatherless and the widow, but he frustrates the ways of the wicked.

Psalm 10:14, 17–18 But you, O God, do see trouble and grief; you consider it to take it in hand. The victim commits himself to you; you are the helper of the fatherless. . . . You hear, O LORD, the desire of the afflicted; you encourage them, and you listen to their cry, defending the fatherless and the oppressed, in order that man, who is of the earth, may terrify no more.

3. **A personal relationship with Jesus Christ is the ultimate family relationship.**

   1 John 3:1 How great is the love the Father has lavished on us, that we should be called children of God! And that is what we are!

   Ephesians 1:4–6 For he chose us in him before the creation of the world to be holy and blameless in his sight. In love he predestined us to be adopted as his sons through Jesus Christ, in accordance with his pleasure and will—to the praise of his glorious grace, which he has freely given us in the One he loves.

   John 3:16 For God so loved the world that he gave his one and only Son, that whoever believes in him shall not perish but have eternal life.

Past Memories

1. **Past triumphs, failures, and losses can entrap one, not allowing freedom to enjoy the present or future.**

   Philippians 3:13–15 Brothers, I do not consider myself yet to have taken hold of it. But one thing I do: Forgetting what is behind and straining toward what is ahead, I press on toward the goal to win the prize for which God has called me heavenward in Christ Jesus. All of us who are mature should take such a view of things. And if on some point you think differently, that too God will make clear to you.

   Isaiah 43:18–19 Forget the former things; do not dwell on the past. See, I am doing a new thing! Now it springs up; do you not perceive it? I am making a way in the desert and streams in the wasteland.

   Luke 9:62 Jesus replied, "No one who puts his hand to the plow and looks back is fit for service in the kingdom of God."

   Isaiah 65:16 Whoever invokes a blessing in the land will do so by the God of truth; he who takes an oath in the land will swear by the God of truth. For the past troubles will be forgotten and hidden from my eyes.

   Ephesians 4:22–23 You were taught, with regard to your former way of life, to put off your old self, which is being corrupted by its deceitful desires; to be made new in the attitude of your minds.

2. **The battle of past memories takes place in the mind.**

   2 Corinthians 10:4–5 The weapons we fight with are not the weapons of the world. On the contrary, they have divine power to demolish strongholds. We demolish arguments and every pretension that sets itself up against the knowledge of God, and we take captive every thought to make it obedient to Christ.

   Philippians 4:8 Finally, brothers, whatever is true, whatever is noble, whatever is right, whatever is pure, whatever is lovely, whatever is admirable—if anything is excellent or praiseworthy—think about such things.

3. **Remember God's provision of the past.**

   Psalm 77:11 I will remember the deeds of the LORD; yes, I will remember your miracles of long ago.

   Joshua 21:45 Not one of all the LORD's good promises to the house of Israel failed; every one was fulfilled.

4. **Concentrate on what God is doing in the present and will do in the future.**

   Isaiah 26:3 You will keep in perfect peace him whose mind is steadfast, because he trusts in you.

   Isaiah 42:10 Sing to the LORD a new song, his praise from the ends of the earth, you who go down to the sea, and all that is in it, you islands, and all who live in them.

   2 Corinthians 5:17 Therefore, if anyone is in Christ, he is a new creation; the old has gone, the new has come!

Premenstrual Syndrome

See also Health, Trials, Depression, Anger

1. **There is no direct mention, but principles of God's sufficiency for any situation will apply.**

   Psalm 91:1–16 He who dwells in the shelter of the Most High will rest in the shadow of the Almighty. I will say of the LORD, "He is my refuge and my fortress, my God, in whom I trust." Surely he will save you from the fowler's snare and from the deadly pestilence. He will cover you with his feathers, and under his wings you will find refuge; his faithfulness will be your shield and rampart. You will not fear the terror of night, nor the arrow that flies by day, nor the pestilence that stalks in the darkness, nor the plague that destroys at midday. A thousand may fall at your side, ten thousand at your right hand, but it will not come near you. You will only observe with your eyes and see the punishment of the wicked. If you make the Most High your dwelling—even the LORD, who is my refuge—then no harm will befall you, no disaster will come near your tent. For he will command his angels concerning you to guard you in all your ways; they will lift you up in their hands, so that you will not strike your foot against a stone. You will tread upon the lion and the cobra; you will trample the great lion and the serpent. "Because he loves me," says the LORD, "I will rescue him; I will protect him, for he acknowledges my name. He will call upon me, and I will answer him; I will be with him in trouble, I will deliver him and honor him. With long life will I satisfy him and show him my salvation."

Matthew 11:28 Come to me, all you who are weary and burdened, and I will give you rest.

2. **God created us—he knows our weaknesses, yet he preserves.**

Isaiah 43:1–2 But now, this is what the LORD says—he who created you, O Jacob, he who formed you, O Israel: "Fear not, for I have redeemed you; I have summoned you by name; you are mine. When you pass through the waters, I will be with you; and when you pass through the rivers, they will not sweep over you. When you walk through the fire, you will not be burned; the flames will not set you ablaze."

3. **Hope in God is help for a depressed, disturbed heart.**

Psalm 42:11 Why are you downcast, O my soul? Why so disturbed within me? Put your hope in God, for I will yet praise him, my Savior and my God.

Psalm 46:1 God is our refuge and strength, an ever-present help in trouble.

4. **PMS can cause conflict within of wanting to do one thing, but doing the opposite. This conflict can lead to sin in speech or actions. The apostle Paul states that Christ is the answer to weakness of mind and body.**

Romans 7:15, 18, 23–25 I do not understand what I do. For what I want to do I do not do, but what I hate I do. . . . I know that nothing good lives in me, that is, in my sinful nature. For I have the desire to do what is good, but I cannot carry it out. . . . But I see another law at work in the members of my body, waging war against the law of my mind and making me a prisoner of the law of sin at work within my members. What a wretched man I am! Who will rescue me from this body of death? Thanks be to God—through Jesus Christ our Lord! So then, I myself in my mind am a slave to God's law, but in the sinful nature a slave to the law of sin.

NOTE: It would be beneficial for the counselee to see a physician.

Prodigal Children

1. **It deeply hurts to have a wayward child.**

   Proverbs 17:25 A foolish son brings grief to his father and bitterness to the one who bore him.

   Proverbs 10:1 A wise son brings joy to his father, but a foolish son grief to his mother.

2. **God understands wayward children and the hurt they bring.**

   Even God has children who do not obey

   Isaiah 1:2 Hear, O heavens! Listen, O earth! For the LORD has spoken: "I reared children and brought them up, but they have rebelled against me."

3. **The battle with the enemy is not ours but God's.**

   Isaiah 49:25 But this is what the LORD says: "Yes, captives will be taken from warriors, and plunder retrieved from the fierce; I will contend with those who contend with you, and your children I will save."

   John 16:33 "I have told you these things, so that in me you may have peace. In this world you will have trouble. But take heart! I have overcome the world."

4. **Strive to keep your own walk with the Lord vital and fresh, not allowing the enemy to use this to cause lack of confidence in God.**

   James 1:2 Consider it pure joy, my brothers, whenever you face trials of many kinds.

God's desire for Israel

Deuteronomy 5:29 Oh, that their hearts would be inclined to fear me and keep all my commands always, so that it might go well with them and their children forever!

Jeremiah 6:16 This is what the LORD says: "Stand at the crossroads and look; ask for the ancient paths, ask where the good way is, and walk in it, and you will find rest for your souls. But you said, 'We will not walk in it.'"

5. **Strive to keep a relationship and lines of communication open so when God gives the opportunity, the child may listen.**

James 5:19–20 My brothers, if one of you should wander from the truth and someone should bring him back, remember this: Whoever turns a sinner from the error of his way will save him from death and cover over a multitude of sins.

Isaiah 58:7 Is it not to share your food with the hungry and to provide the poor wanderer with shelter—when you see the naked, to clothe him, and not to turn away from your own flesh and blood?

Proverbs 29:11 A fool gives full vent to his anger, but a wise man keeps himself under control.

Proverbs 20:3 It is to a man's honor to avoid strife, but every fool is quick to quarrel.

1 Peter 4:8 Above all, love each other deeply, because love covers over a multitude of sins.

Proverbs 26:4–5 Do not answer a fool according to his folly, or you will be like him yourself. Answer a fool according to his folly, or he will be wise in his own eyes.

Galatians 5:22–23 But the fruit of the Spirit is love, joy, peace, patience, kindness, goodness, faithfulness, gentleness and self-control. Against such things there is no law.

Psalm 37:8 Refrain from anger and turn from wrath; do not fret—it leads only to evil.

6. The reality of turning one's back on God.

There are consequences for sin

Proverbs 11:21 Be sure of this: The wicked will not go unpunished, but those who are righteous will go free.

Galatians 6:7 Do not be deceived: God cannot be mocked. A man reaps what he sows.

God forgives rebellion

Daniel 9:9 The Lord our God is merciful and forgiving, even though we have rebelled against him.

Proverbs 28:13 He who conceals his sins does not prosper, but whoever confesses and renounces them finds mercy.

God is the only solution

Isaiah 48:18 If only you had paid attention to my commands, your peace would have been like a river, your righteousness like the waves of the sea.

Isaiah 50:10 Who among you fears the LORD and obeys the word of his servant? Let him who walks in the dark, who has no light, trust in the name of the LORD and rely on his God.

7. Pray constantly for the child, not necessarily for what is wanted as a parent, but what God wants for the child's life.

Romans 8:26 In the same way, the Spirit helps us in our weakness. We do not know what we ought to pray for, but the Spirit himself intercedes for us with groans that words cannot express.

Psalm 63:6 On my bed I remember you; I think of you through the watches of the night.

Matthew 7:7–11 Ask and it will be given to you; seek and you will find; knock and the door will be opened to you. For everyone who asks receives; he who seeks finds; and to him who knocks, the door will be opened. Which of you, if his son asks for bread, will give him a stone? Or if he asks for a fish, will give him a snake? If you, then, though you are evil, know how to give good gifts to your children, how much more will your Father in heaven give good gifts to those who ask him!

Christ's example

John 17:9 I pray for them. I am not praying for the world, but for those you have given me, for they are yours.

Hannah's prayer

1 Samuel 1:27–28 I prayed for this child, and the LORD has granted me what I asked of him. So now I give him to the LORD. For his whole life he will be given over to the LORD.

8. **Hope must always be kept in a loving God who desires to restore that child.**

Jeremiah 32:27 I am the LORD, the God of all mankind. Is anything too hard for me?

Lamentations 3:25–26 The LORD is good to those whose hope is in him, to the one who seeks him; it is good to wait quietly for the salvation of the LORD.

Old Testament hope for Israel

Jeremiah 31:7 This is what the LORD says: "Sing with joy for Jacob; shout for the foremost of the nations. Make your praises heard, and say, 'O LORD, save your people, the remnant of Israel.'"

9. **Do not let the world discourage—anticipate what God can do.**

Luke 15:20 So he got up and went to his father. But while he was still a long way off, his father saw him and was filled with compassion for him; he ran to his son, threw his arms around him and kissed him.

143

Romans 15:13 May the God of hope fill you with all joy and peace as you trust in him, so that you may overflow with hope by the power of the Holy Spirit.

Jeremiah 29:11 "For I know the plans I have for you," declares the LORD, "plans to prosper you and not to harm you, plans to give you hope and a future."

Jeremiah 3:22 "Return, faithless people; I will cure you of backsliding." "Yes, we will come to you, for you are the LORD our God."

Prostitution

See also Repentance and Forgiveness

1. **Prostitution is a sinful way of life and violates God's standards.**

   Proverbs 23:27–28 For a prostitute is a deep pit and a wayward wife is a narrow well. Like a bandit she lies in wait, and multiplies the unfaithful among men.

   1 Corinthians 6:15–17 Do you not know that your bodies are members of Christ himself? Shall I then take the members of Christ and unite them with a prostitute? Never! Do you not know that he who unites himself with a prostitute is one with her in body? For it is said, "The two will become one flesh." But he who unites himself with the Lord is one with him in spirit.

   Many references in the Book of Proverbs

2. **Confession and repentance are the first steps to freedom.**

   Proverbs 28:13 He who conceals his sins does not prosper, but whoever confesses and renounces them finds mercy.

   Romans 6:6 For we know that our old self was crucified with him so that the body of sin might be done away with, that we should no longer be slaves to sin.

Psalm 141:4 Let not my heart be drawn to what is evil, to take part in wicked deeds with men who are evildoers; let me not eat of their delicacies.

3. **Change in lifestyle and right relationship with God anchors freedom.**

    2 Corinthians 5:17 Therefore, if anyone is in Christ, he is a new creation; the old has gone, the new has come!

    Romans 6:19 I put this in human terms because you are weak in your natural selves. Just as you used to offer the parts of your body in slavery to impurity and to ever-increasing wickedness, so now offer them in slavery to righteousness leading to holiness.

    Galatians 6:7–8 Do not be deceived: God cannot be mocked. A man reaps what he sows. The one who sows to please his sinful nature, from that nature will reap destruction; the one who sows to please the Spirit, from the Spirit will reap eternal life.

4. **God's work and evidence of change in the life of one prostitute:**

    Rahab's background: Joshua 2:1–21

    Joshua 6:22–25 Joshua said to the two men who had spied out the land, "Go into the prostitute's house and bring her out and all who belong to her, in accordance with your oath to her." So the young men who had done the spying went in and brought out Rahab, her father and mother and brothers and all who belonged to her. They brought out her entire family and put them in a place outside the camp of Israel. Then they burned the whole city and everything in it, but they put the silver and gold and the articles of bronze and iron into the treasury of the LORD's house. But Joshua spared Rahab the prostitute, with her family and all who belonged to her, because she hid the men Joshua had sent as spies to Jericho— and she lives among the Israelites to this day.

    Hebrews 11:31 By faith the prostitute Rahab, because she welcomed the spies, was not killed with those who were disobedient.

Psychics/Occult/Satan

1. **Satan uses demons in an attempt to defeat the Christian.**

   Ephesians 6:11–12 Put on the full armor of God so that you can take your stand against the devil's schemes. For our struggle is not against flesh and blood, but against the rulers, against the authorities, against the powers of this dark world and against the spiritual forces of evil in the heavenly realms.

2. **God forbids any dealing with the occult.**

   Deuteronomy 18:10–12 Let no one be found among you who sacrifices his son or daughter in the fire, who practices divination or sorcery, interprets omens, engages in witchcraft, or casts spells, or who is a medium or spiritist or who consults the dead. Anyone who does these things is detestable to the LORD, and because of these detestable practices the LORD your God will drive out those nations before you.

   Galatians 5:19–21 The acts of the sinful nature are obvious: sexual immorality, impurity and debauchery; idolatry and witchcraft; hatred, discord, jealousy, fits of rage, selfish ambition, dissensions, factions and envy; drunkenness, orgies, and the like. I warn you, as I did before, that those who live like this will not inherit the kingdom of God.

3. **The enemy seeks our destruction.**

   1 Peter 5:8 Be self-controlled and alert. Your enemy the devil prowls around like a roaring lion looking for someone to devour.

4. **There should be no trying to contact those who have died.**

   Isaiah 8:19 When men tell you to consult mediums and spiritists, who whisper and mutter, should not a people inquire of their God? Why consult the dead on behalf of the living?

5. **The believer's defense against Satan.**

   Be on guard

   1 Peter 5:8 Be self-controlled and alert. Your enemy the devil prowls around like a roaring lion looking for someone to devour.

   We must take a stand

   James 4:7 Submit yourselves, then, to God. Resist the devil, and he will flee from you.

   Do not speak contemptuously of Satan

   Jude 1:8–9 In the very same way, these dreamers pollute their own bodies, reject authority and slander celestial beings. But even the archangel Michael, when he was disputing with the devil about the body of Moses, did not dare to bring a slanderous accusation against him, but said, "The Lord rebuke you!"

6. **God offers power against evil.**

   Ephesians 6:10–18 Finally, be strong in the Lord and in his mighty power. Put on the full armor of God so that you can take your stand against the devil's schemes. For our struggle is not against flesh and blood, but against the rulers, against the authorities, against the powers of this dark world and against the spiritual forces of evil in the heavenly realms. Therefore put on the full armor of God, so that when the day of evil comes, you may be able to stand your ground, and after you have done everything, to stand. Stand firm then, with the belt of truth buckled around your waist, with the breastplate of righteousness in place, and with your feet fitted with the readiness that comes from the gospel of peace. In addition to all this, take up the shield of faith, with which you can extinguish all the flaming arrows of the evil one. Take the helmet of salvation and the sword of the Spirit, which is the word of God. And pray in the Spirit on all occasions with all kinds of prayers and requests. With this in mind, be alert and always keep on praying for all the saints.

1 John 4:4 You, dear children, are from God and have overcome them, because the one who is in you is greater than the one who is in the world.

Quiet Time

1. **Spending time daily in God's Word is vital.**

   Deuteronomy 32:47 They are not just idle words for you—they are your life.

   Psalm 42:1–2 As the deer pants for streams of water, so my soul pants for you, O God. My soul thirsts for God, for the living God. When can I go and meet with God?

   Joshua 1:8 Do not let this Book of the Law depart from your mouth; meditate on it day and night, so that you may be careful to do everything written in it. Then you will be prosperous and successful.

   2 Timothy 3:16–17 All Scripture is God-breathed and is useful for teaching, rebuking, correcting and training in righteousness, so that the man of God may be thoroughly equipped for every good work.

   Psalm 63:1 O God, you are my God, earnestly I seek you; my soul thirsts for you, my body longs for you, in a dry and weary land where there is no water.

   Isaiah 40:8 The grass withers and the flowers fall, but the word of our God stands forever.

   Matthew 6:33 But seek first his kingdom and his righteousness, and all these things will be given to you as well.

Psalm 130:6 My soul waits for the Lord more than watchmen wait for the morning, more than watchmen wait for the morning.

Psalm 34:8 Taste and see that the LORD is good; blessed is the man who takes refuge in him.

2. **Spending time daily in prayer is vital.**

Psalm 5:3 In the morning, O LORD, you hear my voice; in the morning I lay my requests before you and wait in expectation.

Jesus' example

Mark 1:35 Very early in the morning, while it was still dark, Jesus got up, left the house and went off to a solitary place, where he prayed.

Battle plan against the enemy

Ephesians 6:18 And pray in the Spirit on all occasions with all kinds of prayers and requests. With this in mind, be alert and always keep on praying for all the saints.

Daniel 6:10 Three times a day he got down on his knees and prayed, giving thanks to his God, just as he had done before.

3. **Include also music and thanksgiving.**

Colossians 3:16 Let the word of Christ dwell in you richly as you teach and admonish one another with all wisdom, and as you sing psalms, hymns and spiritual songs with gratitude in your hearts to God.

4. **Time in God's Word gives guidance.**

Isaiah 55:11 So is my word that goes out from my mouth: It will not return to me empty, but will accomplish what I desire and achieve the purpose for which I sent it.

Psalm 119:105 Your word is a lamp to my feet and a light for my path.

Jeremiah 17:8 He will be like a tree planted by the water that sends out its roots by the stream. It does not fear when heat comes;

its leaves are always green. It has no worries in a year of drought and never fails to bear fruit.

Psalm 19:9–11 The fear of the LORD is pure, enduring forever. The ordinances of the LORD are sure and altogether righteous. They are more precious than gold, than much pure gold; they are sweeter than honey, than honey from the comb. By them is your servant warned; in keeping them there is great reward.

Psalm 16:8 I have set the LORD always before me. Because he is at my right hand, I will not be shaken.

Rape

See also Past Memories and Fear

1. **When a rape happened God did not place blame on the woman.**

   Deuteronomy 22:26 Do nothing to the girl; she has committed no sin deserving death. This case is like that of someone who attacks and murders his neighbor.

2. **When evil happens, courts and laws may not always be able to provide punishment, but ultimately God will.**

   2 Thessalonians 1:5–7 All this is evidence that God's judgment is right, and as a result you will be counted worthy of the kingdom of God, for which you are suffering. God is just: He will pay back trouble to those who trouble you and give relief to you who are troubled, and to us as well. This will happen when the Lord Jesus is revealed from heaven in blazing fire with his powerful angels.

   Luke 18:6–8 And the Lord said, "Listen to what the unjust judge says. And will not God bring about justice for his chosen ones, who cry out to him day and night? Will he keep putting them off? I tell you, he will see that they get justice, and quickly. However, when the Son of Man comes, will he find faith on the earth?"

   Deuteronomy 32:35 It is mine to avenge; I will repay. In due time their foot will slip; their day of disaster is near and their doom rushes upon them.

3. **Cling to solace in Jesus Christ.**

   1 John 4:4 You, dear children, are from God and have overcome them, because the one who is in you is greater than the one who is in the world.

   Psalm 34:18–19 The LORD is close to the brokenhearted and saves those who are crushed in spirit. A righteous man may have many troubles, but the LORD delivers him from them all.

   Hebrews 12:2–3 Let us fix our eyes on Jesus, the author and perfecter of our faith, who for the joy set before him endured the cross, scorning its shame, and sat down at the right hand of the throne of God. Consider him who endured such opposition from sinful men, so that you will not grow weary and lose heart.

   Isaiah 41:9–10 I took you from the ends of the earth, from its farthest corners I called you. I said, 'You are my servant'; I have chosen you and have not rejected you. So do not fear, for I am with you; do not be dismayed, for I am your God. I will strengthen you and help you; I will uphold you with my righteous right hand.

   Deuteronomy 31:6 Be strong and courageous. Do not be afraid or terrified because of them, for the LORD your God goes with you; he will never leave you nor forsake you.

NOTE: It would be beneficial for the counselee to see a physician if not already done.

Role of the Woman

See also Career, Discipleship, Empty Nest, Marriage, Mothering, Sex Life, Submission, Vanity

1. **Woman was equally created in the image of God.**

   Genesis 1:27 So God created man in his own image, in the image of God he created him; male and female he created them.

2. **God's design for a woman's role is to function under the leadership of man.**

   1 Corinthians 11:3–15 Now I want you to realize that the head of every man is Christ, and the head of the woman is man, and the head of Christ is God. Every man who prays or prophesies with his head covered dishonors his head. And every woman who prays or prophesies with her head uncovered dishonors her head—it is just as though her head were shaved. If a woman does not cover her head, she should have her hair cut off; and if it is a disgrace for a woman to have her hair cut or shaved off, she should cover her head. A man ought not to cover his head, since he is the image and glory of God; but the woman is the glory of man. For man did not come from woman, but woman from man; neither was man created for woman, but woman for man. For this reason, and because of the angels, the woman ought to have a sign of authority on her head. In the Lord, however, woman is not independent of man, nor is man independent of woman. For as woman came from man, so also man is born of woman. But everything comes from God. Judge for yourselves: Is it proper for a woman to pray to God with her head uncovered? Does not the very nature of things teach you that if a man has long hair, it is a disgrace to him, but that if a woman has long hair, it is her glory? For long hair is given to her as a covering.

3. **Note these guidelines for women in worship.**

Refers to teaching and preaching of men

1 Corinthians 14:33–35 For God is not a God of disorder but of peace. As in all the congregations of the saints, women should remain silent in the churches. They are not allowed to speak, but must be in submission, as the Law says. If they want to inquire about something, they should ask their own husbands at home; for it is disgraceful for a woman to speak in the church.

1 Timothy 2:9–15 I also want women to dress modestly, with decency and propriety, not with braided hair or gold or pearls or expensive clothes, but with good deeds, appropriate for women who profess to worship God. A woman should learn in quietness and full submission. I do not permit a woman to teach or to have authority over a man; she must be silent. For Adam was formed first, then Eve. And Adam was not the one deceived; it was the woman who was deceived and became a sinner. But women will be saved through childbearing—if they continue in faith, love and holiness with propriety.

4. **Guidelines to unmarried women.**

1 Corinthians 7:25–26, 28 Now about virgins: I have no command from the Lord, but I give a judgment as one who by the Lord's mercy is trustworthy. Because of the present crisis, I think that it is good for you to remain as you are. . . . But if you do marry, you have not sinned; and if a virgin marries, she has not sinned.

5. **Guidelines for wives.**

The example of the capable, godly wife

Proverbs 31:10–12, 28–31 A wife of noble character who can find? She is worth far more than rubies. Her husband has full confidence in her and lacks nothing of value. She brings him good, not harm, all the days of her life. . . . Her children arise and call her blessed; her husband also, and he praises her: "Many women do noble things, but you surpass them all." Charm is deceptive, and beauty is fleeting; but a woman who fears the Lord is to be praised. Give her the reward she has earned, and let her works bring her praise at the city gate.

For further reference see Proverbs 31:13–17.
See also Marriage, Submission

6. **Guidelines for teaching other women.**

Titus 2:3–5 Likewise, teach the older women to be reverent in the way they live, not to be slanderers or addicted to much wine, but to teach what is good. Then they can train the younger women to love their husbands and children, to be self-controlled and pure, to be busy at home, to be kind, and to be subject to their husbands, so that no one will malign the word of God.

Self-Worth

1. **God's view of our worth.**

   John 3:16 For God so loved the world that he gave his one and only Son, that whoever believes in him shall not perish but have eternal life.

   Romans 8:28–29 And we know that in all things God works for the good of those who love him, who have been called according to his purpose. For those God foreknew he also predestined to be conformed to the likeness of his Son, that he might be the firstborn among many brothers.

2. **Biblical example of struggle with self-worth.**

   Job 9:21 Although I am blameless, I have no concern for myself; I despise my own life.

3. **We find our significance not in ourselves, but in our relationship to God.**

   James 4:10 Humble yourselves before the Lord, and he will lift you up.

   Micah 6:8 He has showed you, O man, what is good. And what does the LORD require of you? To act justly and to love mercy and to walk humbly with your God.

4. **Knowing God is what makes life meaningful.**

   Ephesians 1:17–19 I keep asking that the God of our Lord Jesus Christ, the glorious Father, may give you the Spirit of wisdom and revelation, so that you may know him better. I pray also that the eyes of your heart may be enlightened in order that you may know the hope to which he has called you, the riches of his glorious inheritance in the saints, and his incomparably great power for us who believe. That power is like the working of his mighty strength.

Ephesians 3:14–20 For this reason I kneel before the Father, from whom his whole family in heaven and on earth derives its name. I pray that out of his glorious riches he may strengthen you with power through his Spirit in your inner being, so that Christ may dwell in your hearts through faith. And I pray that you, being rooted and established in love, may have power, together with all the saints, to grasp how wide and long and high and deep is the love of Christ, and to know this love that surpasses knowledge—that you may be filled to the measure of all the fullness of God. Now to him who is able to do immeasurably more than all we ask or imagine, according to his power that is at work within us . . .

Philippians 3:8–10 What is more, I consider everything a loss compared to the surpassing greatness of knowing Christ Jesus my Lord, for whose sake I have lost all things. I consider them rubbish, that I may gain Christ and be found in him, not having a righteousness of my own that comes from the law, but that which is through faith in Christ—the righteousness that comes from God and is by faith. I want to know Christ and the power of his resurrection and the fellowship of sharing in his sufferings, becoming like him in his death.

Jeremiah 9:23–24 This is what the LORD says: "Let not the wise man boast of his wisdom or the strong man boast of his strength or the rich man boast of his riches, but let him who boasts boast about this: that he understands and knows me, that I am the LORD, who exercises kindness, justice and righteousness on earth, for in these I delight," declares the LORD.

5. **We are not to fall into a trap of relying on self.**

   2 Corinthians 1:8–9 We do not want you to be uninformed, brothers, about the hardships we suffered in the province of Asia. We were under great pressure, far beyond our ability to endure, so that we despaired even of life. Indeed, in our hearts we felt the sentence of death. But this happened that we might not rely on ourselves but on God, who raises the dead.

6. **Be careful not to allow pride to enter into a view of self.**

Psalm 10:4 In his pride the wicked does not seek him; in all his thoughts there is no room for God.

Isaiah 2:11–12 The eyes of the arrogant man will be humbled and the pride of men brought low; the LORD alone will be exalted in that day. The LORD Almighty has a day in store for all the proud and lofty, for all that is exalted (and they will be humbled).

2 Corinthians 10:12 We do not dare to classify or compare ourselves with some who commend themselves. When they measure themselves by themselves and compare themselves with themselves, they are not wise.

Sex Life

See also Marriage, Submission

1. **Sexual intimacy in marriage is God's design. Creation as male and female was his plan.**

   Genesis 2:24 For this reason a man will leave his father and mother and be united to his wife, and they will become one flesh.

   Genesis 1:27 In the image of God he created him; male and female he created them.

2. **The husband is responsible to satisfy the wife sexually, and the wife is responsible to satisfy her husband.**

   1 Corinthians 7:3 The husband should fulfill his marital duty to his wife, and likewise the wife to her husband.

3. **Sexual intimacy needs to be constant in marriage, unless both agree to postpone for prayer.**

   1 Corinthians 7:4 The wife's body does not belong to her alone but also to her husband. In the same way, the husband's body does not belong to him alone but also to his wife.

   Philippians 2:3–4 Do nothing out of selfish ambition or vain conceit, but in humility consider others better than yourselves. Each of you should look not only to your own interests, but also to the interests of others.

4. **Being deprived of sexual intimacy provides opportunity for temptation.**

    1 Corinthians 7:5 Do not deprive each other except by mutual consent and for a time, so that you may devote yourselves to prayer. Then come together again so that Satan will not tempt you because of your lack of self-control.

5. **Sexual relations need to be between a married couple alone.**

    Hebrews 13:4 Marriage should be honored by all, and the marriage bed kept pure, for God will judge the adulterer and all the sexually immoral.

6. **Sexual activity is seen as beautiful and to be delighted in by the couple.**

    Proverbs 5:18–19 May your fountain be blessed, and may you rejoice in the wife of your youth. A loving doe, a graceful deer— may her breasts satisfy you always, may you ever be captivated by her love.

    Genesis 26:8 When Isaac had been there a long time, Abimelech king of the Philistines looked down from a window and saw Isaac caressing his wife Rebekah.

    Book of Song of Solomon

Sexual Purity

See also Sex Life

1. **Sexual immorality is sinful and needs to be avoided.**

   Romans 13:14 Rather, clothe yourselves with the Lord Jesus Christ, and do not think about how to gratify the desires of the sinful nature.

   James 1:21 Therefore, get rid of all moral filth and the evil that is so prevalent and humbly accept the word planted in you, which can save you.

   1 Thessalonians 4:3–6 It is God's will that you should be sanctified: that you should avoid sexual immorality; that each of you should learn to control his own body in a way that is holy and honorable, not in passionate lust like the heathen, who do not know God; and that in this matter no one should wrong his brother or take advantage of him. The Lord will punish men for all such sins, as we have already told you and warned you.

   Galatians 5:19–21 The acts of the sinful nature are obvious: sexual immorality, impurity and debauchery; idolatry and witchcraft; hatred, discord, jealousy, fits of rage, selfish ambition, dissensions, factions and envy; drunkenness, orgies, and the like. I warn you, as I did before, that those who live like this will not inherit the kingdom of God.

2. **Our bodies belong to God and need to be pure.**

   1 Corinthians 6:19–20 Do you not know that your body is a temple of the Holy Spirit, who is in you, whom you have received from God? You are not your own; you were bought at a price. Therefore honor God with your body.

3. **Do not even get close to sexual impurity.**

   Ephesians 5:3 But among you there must not be even a hint of sexual immorality, or of any kind of impurity, or of greed, because these are improper for God's holy people.

   Proverbs 6:27 Can a man scoop fire into his lap without his clothes being burned?

4. **Be totally pure.**

   Leviticus 19:2 Speak to the entire assembly of Israel and say to them: "Be holy because I, the LORD your God, am holy."

   1 Peter 1:16 For it is written: "Be holy, because I am holy."

   James 1:27 Religion that God our Father accepts as pure and faultless is this: . . . to keep oneself from being polluted by the world.

5. **Do not submit to pressure sexually or in any other area.**

   Isaiah 51:7 Hear me, you who know what is right, you people who have my law in your hearts: Do not fear the reproach of men or be terrified by their insults.

6. **Each individual has a choice to stay pure.**

   1 Peter 2:11 Dear friends, I urge you, as aliens and strangers in the world, to abstain from sinful desires, which war against your soul.

   James 1:14 But each one is tempted when, by his own evil desire, he is dragged away and enticed.

7. **Guard purity of the mind as well as the body.**

   Matthew 5:28 But I tell you that anyone who looks at a woman lustfully has already committed adultery with her in his heart.

Job 31:1 I made a covenant with my eyes not to look lustfully at a girl.

8. **Protecting purity in marriage begins long before the marriage.**

   Hebrews 13:4 Marriage should be honored by all, and the marriage bed kept pure, for God will judge the adulterer and all the sexually immoral.

9. **Avoid immorality by pursuing what is pure.**

   2 Timothy 2:22 Flee the evil desires of youth, and pursue righteousness, faith, love and peace, along with those who call on the Lord out of a pure heart.

   Colossians 3:5–10 Put to death, therefore, whatever belongs to your earthly nature: sexual immorality, impurity, lust, evil desires and greed, which is idolatry. Because of these, the wrath of God is coming. You used to walk in these ways, in the life you once lived. But now you must rid yourselves of all such things as these: anger, rage, malice, slander, and filthy language from your lips. Do not lie to each other, since you have taken off your old self with its practices and have put on the new self, which is being renewed in knowledge in the image of its Creator.

   Romans 8:5–6 Those who live according to the sinful nature have their minds set on what that nature desires; but those who live in accordance with the Spirit have their minds set on what the Spirit desires. The mind of sinful man is death, but the mind controlled by the Spirit is life and peace.

10. **Be determined and committed to stand strong with God's help.**

   Isaiah 50:7 Because the Sovereign LORD helps me, I will not be disgraced. Therefore have I set my face like flint, and I know I will not be put to shame.

For further reference see Proverbs, especially chapters 4, 5, 7, 9.

Singleness

See also Dating, Sexual Purity

1. **Singleness—the gift of living undivided before the Lord.**

   1 Corinthians 7:25–35 Now about virgins: I have no command from the Lord, but I give a judgment as one who by the Lord's mercy is trustworthy. Because of the present crisis, I think that it is good for you to remain as you are. Are you married? Do not seek a divorce. Are you unmarried? Do not look for a wife. But if you do marry, you have not sinned; and if a virgin marries, she has not sinned. But those who marry will face many troubles in this life, and I want to spare you this. What I mean, brothers, is that the time is short. From now on those who have wives should live as if they had none; those who mourn, as if they did not; those who are happy, as if they were not; those who buy something, as if it were not theirs to keep; those who use the things of the world, as if not engrossed in them. For this world in its present form is passing away. I would like you to be free from concern. An unmarried man is concerned about the Lord's affairs—how he can please the Lord. But a married man is concerned about the affairs of this world—how he can please his wife—and his interests are divided. An unmarried woman or virgin is concerned about the Lord's affairs: Her aim is to be devoted to the Lord in both body and spirit. But a married woman is concerned about the affairs of this world—how she can please her husband. I am saying this for your own good, not to restrict you, but that you may live in a right way in undivided devotion to the Lord.

Matthew 19:11–12 Jesus replied, "Not everyone can accept this word, but only those to whom it has been given. For some are eunuchs because they were born that way; others were made that way by men; and others have renounced marriage because of the kingdom of heaven. The one who can accept this should accept it."

Contentment in singleness

1. **God's personal interest.**

   Isaiah 41:9–10 'You are my servant'; I have chosen you and have not rejected you. So do not fear, for I am with you; do not be dismayed, for I am your God. I will strengthen you and help you; I will uphold you with my righteous right hand.

   Jeremiah 29:11 "For I know the plans I have for you," declares the LORD, "plans to prosper you and not to harm you, plans to give you hope and a future."

2. **God's commitment.**

   Isaiah 54:5 For your Maker is your husband—the LORD Almighty is his name—the Holy One of Israel is your Redeemer; he is called the God of all the earth.

   Isaiah 40:31 But those who hope in the LORD will renew their strength. They will soar on wings like eagles; they will run and not grow weary, they will walk and not be faint.

   Romans 8:38–39 For I am convinced that neither death nor life, neither angels nor demons, neither the present nor the future, nor any powers, neither height nor depth, nor anything else in all creation, will be able to separate us from the love of God that is in Christ Jesus our Lord.

3. **Contentment with self.**

   Psalm 139:13–14 For you created my inmost being; you knit me together in my mother's womb. I praise you because I am fearfully and wonderfully made; your works are wonderful, I know that full well.

1 Peter 3:3–4 Your beauty should not come from outward adornment, such as braided hair and the wearing of gold jewelry and fine clothes. Instead, it should be that of your inner self, the unfading beauty of a gentle and quiet spirit, which is of great worth in God's sight.

Philippians 4:12–13 I know what it is to be in need, and I know what it is to have plenty. I have learned the secret of being content in any and every situation, whether well fed or hungry, whether living in plenty or in want. I can do everything through him who gives me strength.

4. **Contentment with intimacy with God.**

Psalm 17:15 And I—in righteousness I will see your face; when I awake, I will be satisfied with seeing your likeness.

Psalm 46:10 "Be still, and know that I am God; I will be exalted among the nations, I will be exalted in the earth."

Psalm 103:2–5 Praise the LORD, O my soul, and forget not all his benefits—who forgives all your sins and heals all your diseases, who redeems your life from the pit and crowns you with love and compassion, who satisfies your desires with good things so that your youth is renewed like the eagle's.

Psalm 4:8 I will lie down and sleep in peace, for you alone, O LORD, make me dwell in safety.

2 Corinthians 12:9 But he said to me, "My grace is sufficient for you, for my power is made perfect in weakness." Therefore I will boast all the more gladly about my weaknesses, so that Christ's power may rest on me.

Psalm 62:5–8 Find rest, O my soul, in God alone; my hope comes from him. He alone is my rock and my salvation; he is my fortress, I will not be shaken. My salvation and my honor depend on God; he is my mighty rock, my refuge. Trust in him at all times, O people; pour out your hearts to him, for God is our refuge.

Psalm 84:11 For the LORD God is a sun and shield; the LORD bestows favor and honor; no good thing does he withhold from those whose walk is blameless.

Jeremiah 31:3 The LORD appeared to us in the past, saying: "I have loved you with an everlasting love; I have drawn you with loving-kindness."

Sleeplessness/Insomnia

1. **We are never alone when we sleep.**

   Psalm 4:8 I will lie down and sleep in peace, for you alone, O LORD, make me dwell in safety.

2. **Even though we face a variety of struggles we can always sleep and rest in God's sovereignty.**

   Psalm 92:2 To proclaim your love in the morning and your faithfulness at night . . .

   Psalm 3:1–8 O LORD, how many are my foes! How many rise up against me! Many are saying of me, "God will not deliver him." But you are a shield around me, O LORD; you bestow glory on me and lift up my head. To the LORD I cry aloud, and he answers me from his holy hill. I lie down and sleep; I wake again, because the LORD sustains me. I will not fear the tens of thousands drawn up against me on every side. Arise, O LORD! Deliver me, O my God! Strike all my enemies on the jaw; break the teeth of the wicked. From the LORD comes deliverance. May your blessing be on your people.

   Psalm 74:16 The day is yours, and yours also the night; you established the sun and moon.

   Matthew 6:33–34 But seek first his kingdom and his righteousness, and all these things will be given to you as well. Therefore do not worry about tomorrow, for tomorrow will worry about itself. Each day has enough trouble of its own.

3. **Be open to God's teaching and instruction even at night.**

Psalm 16:7–9 I will praise the LORD, who counsels me; even at night my heart instructs me. I have set the LORD always before me. Because he is at my right hand, I will not be shaken. Therefore my heart is glad and my tongue rejoices; my body also will rest secure.

Isaiah 26:9 My soul yearns for you in the night; in the morning my spirit longs for you. When your judgments come upon the earth, the people of the world learn righteousness.

4. **When sleep evades, spend time in prayer and thanksgiving.**

Psalm 63:6–8 On my bed I remember you; I think of you through the watches of the night. Because you are my help, I sing in the shadow of your wings. My soul clings to you; your right hand upholds me.

5. **When sleep evades, read or quote Scripture.**

Psalm 1:2 But his delight is in the law of the LORD, and on his law he meditates day and night.

6. **When sleep evades, sing, quote songs, or pray.**

Psalm 42:8 By day the LORD directs his love, at night his song is with me—a prayer to the God of my life.

Psalm 77:6 I remembered my songs in the night. My heart mused and my spirit inquired. . . .

NOTE: It would be beneficial to have the counselee see a physician.

Spiritual Gifts

1. **Each believer has at least one spiritual gift.**

   1 Peter 4:10–11 Each one should use whatever gift he has received to serve others, faithfully administering God's grace in its various forms. If anyone speaks, he should do it as one speaking the very words of God. If anyone serves, he should do it with the strength God provides, so that in all things God may be praised through Jesus Christ. To him be the glory and the power for ever and ever. Amen.

   1 Corinthians 7:7 I wish that all men were as I am. But each man has his own gift from God; one has this gift, another has that.

2. **Believers need to know what spiritual gifts are available so they can be equipped to serve the body of Christ.**

   Romans 12:6–8 We have different gifts, according to the grace given us. If a man's gift is prophesying, let him use it in proportion to his faith. If it is serving, let him serve; if it is teaching, let him teach; if it is encouraging, let him encourage; if it is contributing to the needs of others, let him give generously; if it is leadership, let him govern diligently; if it is showing mercy, let him do it cheerfully.

   1 Corinthians 12:4–11 There are different kinds of gifts, but the same Spirit. There are different kinds of service, but the same Lord. There are different kinds of working, but the same God works all of them in all men. Now to each one the manifestation of the Spirit is given for the common good. To one there is given through the Spirit the message of wisdom, to another the message of knowledge by means of the same Spirit, to another faith by the same Spirit, to another gifts of healing by that one Spirit, to another miraculous powers, to another prophecy, to another distinguishing between spirits, to another speaking in different kinds of tongues, and to still another the interpretation of tongues. All these are the work of one and the same Spirit, and he gives them to each one, just as he determines.

Ephesians 4:7–11 But to each one of us grace has been given as Christ apportioned it. This is why it says: "When he ascended on high, he led captives in his train and gave gifts to men.". . . It was he who gave some to be apostles, some to be prophets, some to be evangelists, and some to be pastors and teachers.

Stillbirth

See also Death/Grief, Miscarriage, God's Will, Trials

1. **This passage is often used to support the belief that infants who have died do go to heaven.**

    2 Samuel 12:18–23 On the seventh day the child died. David's servants were afraid to tell him that the child was dead, for they thought, "While the child was still living, we spoke to David but he would not listen to us. How can we tell him the child is dead? He may do something desperate." David noticed that his servants were whispering among themselves and he realized the child was dead. "Is the child dead?" he asked. "Yes," they replied, "he is dead." Then David got up from the gound. After he had washed, put on lotions and changed his clothes, he went into the house of the LORD and worshiped. Then he went to his own house, and at his request they served him food, and he ate. His servants asked him, "Why are you acting this way? While the child was alive, you fasted and wept, but now that the child is dead, you get up and eat!" He answered, "While the child was still alive, I fasted and wept. I thought, 'Who Knows? The Lord may be gracious to me and let the child live.' But now that he is dead, why should I fast? Can I bring him back again? I will go to him, but he will not return to me."

2. **God is involved and knows the unborn.**

    Isaiah 49:1 Listen to me, you islands; hear this, you distant nations: Before I was born the LORD called me; from my birth he has made mention of my name.

Jeremiah 1:4–5 The word of the LORD came to me, saying, "Before I formed you in the womb I knew you, before you were born I set you apart; I appointed you as a prophet to the nations."

Jeremiah 20:17 For he did not kill me in the womb, with my mother as my grave, her womb enlarged forever.

Psalm 139:15–16 My frame was not hidden from you when I was made in the secret place. When I was woven together in the depths of the earth, your eyes saw my unformed body. All the days ordained for me were written in your book before one of them came to be.

Ecclesiastes 11:5 As you do not know the path of the wind, or how the body is formed in a mother's womb, so you cannot understand the work of God, the Maker of all things.

Submission

1. **Submission is for all believers.**

   Ephesians 5:21 Submit to one another out of reverence for Christ.

   Philippians 2:5 Your attitude should be the same as that of Christ Jesus.

   Hebrews 13:17 Obey your leaders and submit to their authority. They keep watch over you as men who must give an account. Obey them so that their work will be a joy, not a burden, for that would be of no advantage to you.

2. **Wives are to submit to their husbands as to the Lord.**

   Ephesians 5:22 Wives, submit to your husbands as to the Lord.

   Colossians 3:18 Wives, submit to your husbands, as is fitting in the Lord.

   1 Corinthians 11:3 Now I want you to realize that the head of every man is Christ, and the head of the woman is man, and the head of Christ is God.

3. **Submission is not difficult when it is in response to a loving husband's leadership.**

   Ephesians 5:25–29, 33 Husbands, love your wives, just as Christ loved the church and gave himself up for her to make her holy, cleansing her by the washing with water through the word, and to present her to himself as a radiant church, without stain or wrinkle or any other blemish, but holy and blameless. In this same way, husbands ought to love their wives as their own bodies. He who loves his wife loves himself. After all, no one ever hated his own body, but he feeds and cares for it, just as Christ does the church. . . . However, each one of you also must love his wife as he loves himself, and the wife must respect her husband.

4. **A woman should not be afraid of submission.**

   1 Peter 3:6 Like Sarah, who obeyed Abraham and called him her master. You are her daughters if you do what is right and do not give way to fear.

5. **Wives need to be submissive to their own husbands.**

   1 Peter 3:5 For this is the way the holy women of the past who put their hope in God used to make themselves beautiful. They were submissive to their own husbands.

6. **Submission does not mean that a wife does not have input. Sarah, the example of submission in 1 Peter 3:6, gave Abraham input which God said he was to follow.**

   Genesis 21:11–12 The matter distressed Abraham greatly because it concerned his son. But God said to him, "Do not be so distressed about the boy and your maidservant. Listen to whatever Sarah tells you, because it is through Isaac that your offspring will be reckoned."

7. **The unsaved husband may come to faith in the Lord as the result of his wife's submission.**

   1 Peter 3:1 Wives, in the same way be submissive to your husbands so that, if any of them do not believe the word, they may be won over without words by the behavior of their wives.

8. **It is the responsibility of older women to teach and exemplify submission to younger women.**

   Titus 2:3–5 Likewise, teach the older women to be reverent in the way they live, not to be slanderers or addicted to much wine, but to teach what is good. Then they can train the younger women to love their husbands and children, to be self-controlled and pure, to be busy at home, to be kind, and to be subject to their husbands, so that no one will malign the word of God.

Television/Movies/Internet/ Reading Material

1. **Do not follow the world's standards—reject what is unseemly or immoral.**

   3 John 1:11 Dear friend, do not imitate what is evil but what is good. Anyone who does what is good is from God. Anyone who does what is evil has not seen God.

   Psalm 101:3 I will set before my eyes no vile thing. The deeds of faithless men I hate; they will not cling to me.

   Galatians 5:19–21 The acts of the sinful nature are obvious: sexual immorality, impurity and debauchery; idolatry and witchcraft; hatred, discord, jealousy, fits of rage, selfish ambition, dissensions, factions and envy; drunkenness, orgies, and the like. I warn you, as I did before, that those who live like this will not inherit the kingdom of God.

   Ephesians 5:4 Nor should there be obscenity, foolish talk or coarse joking, which are out of place, but rather thanksgiving.

   Colossians 2:8 See to it that no one takes you captive through hollow and deceptive philosophy, which depends on human tradition and the basic principles of this world rather than on Christ.

   Romans 8:5–6 Those who live according to the sinful nature have their minds set on what that nature desires; but those who live in accordance with the Spirit have their minds set on what the Spirit desires. The mind of sinful man is death, but the mind controlled by the Spirit is life and peace.

Isaiah 5:20 Woe to those who call evil good and good evil, who put darkness for light and light for darkness, who put bitter for sweet and sweet for bitter.

2. **Actively pursue what is right.**

Colossians 3:1–4 Since, then, you have been raised with Christ, set your hearts on things above, where Christ is seated at the right hand of God. Set your minds on things above, not on earthly things. For you died, and your life is now hidden with Christ in God. When Christ, who is your life, appears, then you also will appear with him in glory.

Colossians 2:6 So then, just as you received Christ Jesus as Lord, continue to live in him.

Philippians 4:8 Finally, brothers, whatever is true, whatever is noble, whatever is right, whatever is pure, whatever is lovely, whatever is admirable—if anything is excellent or praiseworthy—think about such things.

Romans 12:1–2 Therefore, I urge you, brothers, in view of God's mercy, to offer your bodies as living sacrifices, holy and pleasing to God—this is your spiritual act of worship. Do not conform any longer to the pattern of this world, but be transformed by the renewing of your mind. Then you will be able to test and approve what God's will is—his good, pleasing and perfect will.

Temptation

1. **The old flesh is responsible for temptation.**

   James 1:14 But each one is tempted when, by his own evil desire, he is dragged away and enticed.

   Romans 7:18 I know that nothing good lives in me, that is, in my sinful nature. For I have the desire to do what is good, but I cannot carry it out.

2. **Temptation in itself is not sin; it is yielding to that temptation that becomes sin.**

   1 Corinthians 10:13 No temptation has seized you except what is common to man. And God is faithful; he will not let you be tempted beyond what you can bear. But when you are tempted, he will also provide a way out so that you can stand up under it.

3. **Christ understands temptation—yet he never sinned.**

   Hebrews 4:15 For we do not have a high priest who is unable to sympathize with our weaknesses, but we have one who has been tempted in every way, just as we are—yet was without sin.

4. **Help can be requested to avoid temptation.**

   Luke 11:4 Forgive us our sins, for we also forgive everyone who sins against us. And lead us not into temptation.

Hebrews 4:16 Let us then approach the throne of grace with confidence, so that we may receive mercy and find grace to help us in our time of need.

5. **Courage is needed, with God's help, to stand strong in temptation.**

James 1:12 Blessed is the man who perseveres under trial, because when he has stood the test, he will receive the crown of life that God has promised to those who love him.

Hebrews 12:1 Therefore, since we are surrounded by such a great cloud of witnesses, let us throw off everything that hinders and the sin that so easily entangles, and let us run with perseverance the race marked out for us.

2 Corinthians 12:9 But he said to me, "My grace is sufficient for you, for my power is made perfect in weakness." Therefore I will boast all the more gladly about my weaknesses, so that Christ's power may rest on me.

Ephesians 6:10–13 Finally, be strong in the Lord and in his mighty power. Put on the full armor of God so that you can take your stand against the devil's schemes. For our struggle is not against flesh and blood, but against the rulers, against the authorities, against the powers of this dark world and against the spiritual forces of evil in the heavenly realms. Therefore put on the full armor of God, so that when the day of evil comes, you may be able to stand your ground, and after you have done everything, to stand.

Proverbs 4:14–15 Do not set foot on the path of the wicked or walk in the way of evil men. Avoid it, do not travel on it; turn from it and go on your way.

1 John 4:4 You, dear children, are from God and have overcome them, because the one who is in you is greater than the one who is in the world.

6. **Lack of sexual intimacy in a marriage can cause sexual temptation.**

1 Corinthians 7:5 Do not deprive each other except by mutual consent and for a time, so that you may devote yourselves to prayer. Then come together again so that Satan will not tempt you because of your lack of self-control.

7. **Caution in helping others flee temptation: do not be caught yourself.**

Galatians 6:1 Brothers, if someone is caught in a sin, you who are spiritual should restore him gently. But watch yourself, or you also may be tempted.

Proverbs 28:10 He who leads the upright along an evil path will fall into his own trap, but the blameless will receive a good inheritance.

1 Timothy 6:9–10 People who want to get rich fall into temptation and a trap and into many foolish and harmful desires that plunge men into ruin and destruction. For the love of money is a root of all kinds of evil. Some people, eager for money, have wandered from the faith and pierced themselves with many griefs.

Training Children

See also Disciplining Children, Mothering

1. **Children need training from early childhood.**

   Psalm 58:3 Even from birth the wicked go astray; from the womb they are wayward and speak lies.

   Genesis 8:21 The LORD smelled the pleasing aroma and said in his heart: "Never again will I curse the ground because of man, even though every inclination of his heart is evil from childhood. And never again will I destroy all living creatures, as I have done."

2. **It is the parents' responsibility to teach their children God's absolute standards.**

   2 Timothy 3:15 And how from infancy you have known the holy Scriptures, which are able to make you wise for salvation through faith in Christ Jesus.

   Deuteronomy 6:6–7, 9 These commandments that I give you today are to be upon your hearts. Impress them on your children. Talk about them when you sit at home and when you walk along the road, when you lie down and when you get up. . . . Write them on the door frames of your houses and on your gates.

Isaiah 54:13 All your sons will be taught by the LORD, and great will be your children's peace.

Psalm 34:11 Come, my children, listen to me; I will teach you the fear of the LORD.

Proverbs 1:8 Listen, my son, to your father's instruction and do not forsake your mother's teaching.

Proverbs 6:20 My son, keep your father's commands and do not forsake your mother's teaching.

3. God's Word is the basis for child training.

James 1:21–25 Therefore, get rid of all moral filth and the evil that is so prevalent and humbly accept the word planted in you, which can save you. Do not merely listen to the word, and so deceive yourselves. Do what it says. Anyone who listens to the word but does not do what it says is like a man who looks at his face in a mirror and, after looking at himself, goes away and immediately forgets what he looks like. But the man who looks intently into the perfect law that gives freedom, and continues to do this, not forgetting what he has heard, but doing it—he will be blessed in what he does.

Psalm 1:1–3 Blessed is the man who does not walk in the counsel of the wicked or stand in the way of sinners or sit in the seat of mockers. But his delight is in the law of the LORD, and on his law he meditates day and night. He is like a tree planted by streams of water, which yields its fruit in season and whose leaf does not wither. Whatever he does prospers.

Psalm 119:9–11 How can a young man keep his way pure? By living according to your word. I seek you with all my heart; do not let me stray from your commands. I have hidden your word in my heart that I might not sin against you.

Psalm 119:105 Your word is a lamp to my feet and a light for my path.

Isaiah 5:20 Woe to those who call evil good and good evil, who put darkness for light and light for darkness, who put bitter for sweet and sweet for bitter.

4. **Parents need to spend time training children.**

Proverbs 22:6 Train a child in the way he should go, and when he is old he will not turn from it.

Ephesians 6:4 Fathers, do not exasperate your children; instead, bring them up in the training and instruction of the Lord.

5. **Discipleship begins at home.**

Deuteronomy 6:6–7 These commandments that I give you today are to be upon your hearts. Impress them on your children. Talk about them when you sit at home and when you walk along the road, when you lie down and when you get up.

6. **Do not cause discouragement.**

Colossians 3:21 Fathers, do not embitter your children, or they will become discouraged.

Ephesians 6:4 Fathers, do not exasperate your children; instead, bring them up in the training and instruction of the Lord.

7. **As parents are to be obedient to God, so children should be obedient to parents.**

1 Peter 1:13–16 Therefore, prepare your minds for action; be self-controlled; set your hope fully on the grace to be given you when Jesus Christ is revealed. As obedient children, do not conform to the evil desires you had when you lived in ignorance. But just as he who called you is holy, so be holy in all you do; for it is written: "Be holy, because I am holy."

Ephesians 6:1 Children, obey your parents in the Lord, for this is right.

Colossians 3:20 Children, obey your parents in everything, for this pleases the Lord.

Trials/Suffering

1. **Trials are to be expected and remind us of the suffering Christ endured.**

   1 Peter 4:12–13 Dear friends, do not be surprised at the painful trial you are suffering, as though something strange were happening to you. But rejoice that you participate in the sufferings of Christ, so that you may be overjoyed when his glory is revealed.

   Romans 8:18–23 I consider that our present sufferings are not worth comparing with the glory that will be revealed in us. The creation waits in eager expectation for the sons of God to be revealed. For the creation was subjected to frustration, not by its own choice, but by the will of the one who subjected it, in hope that the creation itself will be liberated from its bondage to decay and brought into the glorious freedom of the children of God. We know that the whole creation has been groaning as in the pains of childbirth right up to the present time. Not only so, but we ourselves, who have the firstfruits of the Spirit, groan inwardly as we wait eagerly for our adoption as sons, the redemption of our bodies.

   John 16:33 "I have told you these things, so that in me you may have peace. In this world you will have trouble. But take heart! I have overcome the world."

2. **A purpose of trials is to strengthen our faith.**

   1 Peter 1:6–7 In this you greatly rejoice, though now for a little while you may have had to suffer grief in all kinds of trials. These have come so that your faith—of greater worth than gold, which perishes even though refined by fire—may be proved genuine and may result in praise, glory and honor when Jesus Christ is revealed.

Job 23:9–11 When he is at work in the north, I do not see him; when he turns to the south, I catch no glimpse of him. But he knows the way that I take; when he has tested me, I will come forth as gold. My feet have closely followed his steps; I have kept to his way without turning aside.

3. **Commands to obey when facing trials.**

   James 5:13 Is any one of you in trouble? He should pray. Is anyone happy? Let him sing songs of praise.

   James 1:2 Consider it pure joy, my brothers, whenever you face trials of many kinds.

   2 Timothy 2:3 Endure hardship with us like a good soldier of Christ Jesus.

4. **Always remember God is sovereign in trials.**

   Jeremiah 10:23 I know, O LORD, that a man's life is not his own; it is not for man to direct his steps.

   Isaiah 43:1–3 But now, this is what the LORD says—he who created you, O Jacob, he who formed you, O Israel: "Fear not, for I have redeemed you; I have summoned you by name; you are mine. When you pass through the waters, I will be with you; and when you pass through the rivers, they will not sweep over you. When you walk through the fire, you will not be burned; the flames will not set you ablaze. For I am the LORD, your God, the Holy One of Israel, your Savior."

   Psalm 23:4 Even though I walk through the valley of the shadow of death, I will fear no evil, for you are with me; your rod and your staff, they comfort me.

5. **God's strength in trials is the solution to strengthening others.**

   2 Corinthians 1:3–4 Praise be to the God and Father of our Lord Jesus Christ, the Father of compassion and the God of all comfort, who comforts us in all our troubles, so that we can comfort those in any trouble with the comfort we ourselves have received from God.

6. **A result of enduring trials is God's reward.**

James 1:12 Blessed is the man who perseveres under trial, because when he has stood the test, he will receive the crown of life that God has promised to those who love him.

2 Corinthians 4:16–18 Therefore we do not lose heart. Though outwardly we are wasting away, yet inwardly we are being renewed day by day. For our light and momentary troubles are achieving for us an eternal glory that far outweighs them all. So we fix our eyes not on what is seen, but on what is unseen. For what is seen is temporary, but what is unseen is eternal.

Trust/Faith

1. **Trust is to be placed ultimately in God alone.**

   Psalm 20:7 Some trust in chariots and some in horses, but we trust in the name of the LORD our God.

   John 14:1 Do not let your hearts be troubled. Trust in God; trust also in me.

2. **We are to trust in God at all times.**

   Psalm 63:8 My soul clings to you; your right hand upholds me.

   Isaiah 26:4 Trust in the LORD forever, for the LORD, the LORD, is the Rock eternal.

   Psalm 26:1 Vindicate me, O LORD, for I have led a blameless life; I have trusted in the LORD without wavering.

3. **We are not to trust in ourselves.** /

   Psalm 49:12–13 But man, despite his riches, does not endure; he is like the beasts that perish. This is the fate of those who trust in themselves, and of their followers, who approve their sayings.

   Proverbs 3:5–6 Trust in the LORD with all your heart and lean not on your own understanding; in all your ways acknowledge him, and he will make your paths straight.

4. **When we are afraid, we are to trust.**

   Psalm 56:3, 11 When I am afraid, I will trust in you. . . . In God I trust; I will not be afraid. What can man do to me?

5. **Love for God and others includes trust.**

   1 Corinthians 13:6–7 Love does not delight in evil but rejoices with the truth. It always protects, always trusts, always hopes, always perseveres.

6. **Results of trusting God.**

   Protection

   Psalm 5:11 But let all who take refuge in you be glad; let them ever sing for joy. Spread your protection over them, that those who love your name may rejoice in you.

   Proverbs 30:5 Every word of God is flawless; he is a shield to those who take refuge in him.

   Psalm 36:7 How priceless is your unfailing love! Both high and low among men find refuge in the shadow of your wings.

   Gladness

   Psalm 64:10 Let the righteous rejoice in the LORD and take refuge in him; let all the upright in heart praise him!

   Peace

   Isaiah 26:3 You will keep in perfect peace him whose mind is steadfast, because he trusts in you.

   Blessing

   Psalm 84:12 O LORD Almighty, blessed is the man who trusts in you.

Jeremiah 17:7 But blessed is the man who trusts in the LORD, whose confidence is in him.

Confidence

Psalm 112:7 He will have no fear of bad news; his heart is steadfast, trusting in the LORD.

Unsaved Spouse

See also Marriage, Submission

1. **Consistent living because of God's grace is required in any believer's life.**

    Titus 2:11–14 For the grace of God that brings salvation has appeared to all men. It teaches us to say "No" to ungodliness and worldly passions, and to live self-controlled, upright and godly lives in this present age, while we wait for the blessed hope—the glorious appearing of our great God and Savior, Jesus Christ, who gave himself for us to redeem us from all wickedness and to purify for himself a people that are his very own, eager to do what is good.

2. **Consistent living because of God's grace as a testimony to an unbelieving husband is encouraged.**

    1 Peter 3:1–6 Wives, in the same way be submissive to your husbands so that, if any of them do not believe the word, they may be won over without words by the behavior of their wives, when they see the purity and reverence of your lives. Your beauty should not come from outward adornment, such as braided hair and the wearing of gold jewelry and fine clothes. Instead, it should be that of your inner self, the unfading beauty of a gentle and quiet spirit, which is of great worth in God's sight. For this is the way the holy women of the past who put their hope in God used to make themselves beautiful. They were submissive to their own husbands, like Sarah, who obeyed Abraham and called him her master. You are her daughters if you do what is right and do not give way to fear.

1 Corinthians 7:12–17 If any brother has a wife who is not a believer and she is willing to live with him, he must not divorce her. And if a woman has a husband who is not a believer and he is willing to live with her, she must not divorce him. For the unbelieving husband has been sanctified through his wife, and the unbelieving wife has been sanctified through her believing husband. Otherwise your children would be unclean, but as it is, they are holy. But if the unbeliever leaves, let him do so. A believing man or woman is not bound in such circumstances; God has called us to live in peace. How do you know, wife, whether you will save your husband? Or, how do you know, husband, whether you will save your wife? Nevertheless, each one should retain the place in life that the Lord assigned to him and to which God has called him. This is the rule I lay down in all the churches.

Vanity/Apparel

1. **Dress needs to be modest, not elaborate or for show.**

   1 Timothy 2:9–10 I also want women to dress modestly, with decency and propriety, not with braided hair or gold or pearls or expensive clothes, but with good deeds, appropriate for women who profess to worship God.

2. **Israel's women were corrected for unbecoming dress.**

   Isaiah 3:16–23 The LORD says, "The women of Zion are haughty, walking along with outstretched necks, flirting with their eyes, tripping along with mincing steps, with ornaments jingling on their ankles. Therefore the Lord will bring sores on the heads of the women of Zion; the LORD will make their scalps bald." In that day the Lord will snatch away their finery: the bangles and headbands and crescent necklaces, the earrings and bracelets and veils, the headdresses and ankle chains and sashes, the perfume bottles and charms, the signet rings and nose rings, the fine robes and the capes and cloaks, the purses and mirrors, and the linen garments and tiaras and shawls.

3. **Concentrate on inner beauty rather than outer beauty.**

   1 Peter 3:3–5 Your beauty should not come from outward adornment, such as braided hair and the wearing of gold jewelry and fine clothes. Instead, it should be that of your inner self, the unfading beauty of a gentle and quiet spirit, which is of great worth in God's sight. For this is the way the holy women of the past who put their hope in God used to make themselves beautiful. They were submissive to their own husbands.

4. **Outward beauty is fleeting.**

Proverbs 31:30 Charm is deceptive, and beauty is fleeting; but a woman who fears the LORD is to be praised.

5. **God sees the heart.**

1 Samuel 16:7 The LORD does not look at the things man looks at. Man looks at the outward appearance, but the LORD looks at the heart.

Luke 16:15 He said to them, "You are the ones who justify yourselves in the eyes of men, but God knows your hearts. What is highly valued among men is detestable in God's sight."

Widows

1. As seen consistently throughout Scripture, God has a loving concern for the care of widows.

   Psalm 68:5 A father to the fatherless, a defender of widows, is God in his holy dwelling.

   James 1:27 Religion that God our Father accepts as pure and faultless is this: to look after orphans and widows in their distress and to keep oneself from being polluted by the world.

   Zechariah 7:10 Do not oppress the widow or the fatherless, the alien or the poor. In your hearts do not think evil of each other.

   Exodus 22:22–24 Do not take advantage of a widow or an orphan. If you do and they cry out to me, I will certainly hear their cry. My anger will be aroused, and I will kill you with the sword; your wives will become widows and your children fatherless.

   Deuteronomy 10:18 He defends the cause of the fatherless and the widow, and loves the alien, giving him food and clothing.

   Jeremiah 22:3 This is what the LORD says: Do what is just and right. Rescue from the hand of his oppressor the one who has been robbed. Do no wrong or violence to the alien, the fatherless or the widow, and do not shed innocent blood in this place.

2. **A widow can trust God for her care.**

Jeremiah 49:11 Leave your orphans; I will protect their lives. Your widows too can trust in me.

Jeremiah 29:13 You will seek me and find me when you seek me with all your heart.

Isaiah 46:4 Even to your old age and gray hairs I am he, I am he who will sustain you. I have made you and I will carry you; I will sustain you and I will rescue you.

Psalm 146:9 The LORD watches over the alien and sustains the fatherless and the widow, but he frustrates the ways of the wicked.

Proverbs 15:25 The LORD tears down the proud man's house but he keeps the widow's boundaries intact.

3. **Biblical examples of widows.**

Naomi—Book of Ruth

Widow of Zarephath—1 Kings 17

Widow with two mites—Mark 12:41–44

Widow of Nain—Luke 7:11–15

Notes

NOTES

NOTES

NOTES

NOTES

NOTES